# HEALTHIER THAN NORMAL

*My Spiritual Victory*

*over*

*Crohn's Disease and Depression*

## By Mike Florak

Published by Mike Florak
Youngstown, Ohio

ISBN 0-9753693-0-X

Dedicated to my friends, family, and God, who stayed beside me every step of the way, and to all of those who suffer from IBD or any other affliction; things will get better if you have faith and determination.

Title: Healthier than Normal

Subtitle: My Spiritual Victory over Crohn's Disease and Depression

Copyright @ 2005 by Mike Florak

Edited by Diane Wilding

Requests for permission to make copies of this work may be mailed to Mike Florak, Mike Florak Enterprises, P.O. Box 2547, Wintersville, OH 43953 or e-mailed to mflorak@ndcis.com, or call 1-888-4FLORAK or 1-888-435-6125.

ISBN 0-9753693-0-X

Published by Mike Florak

Printed in the United States of America

# What's Being Said about This Book

*"An inspirational and brutally honest real-life story of how one man has overcome the mental and physical struggles of a disease that nobody wants to talk about—a 'must read' if you or any one in your circle of family or friends has had the misfortune of having to deal with Crohn's disease."*

**Mark Bercik, president, America Sports Publishing**

*"Mike Florak is not only an excellent college baseball coach, but he's also an outstanding person!* Healthier than Normal *is the story about his ability to battle through his numerous health problems and still continue to excel in his chosen profession. It is a tremendous example to all."*

**John Caparanis, ESPN Radio 1240, Youngstown, Ohio**

*"When I met Mike Florak, I knew nothing of Crohn's disease and what it means to have this illness. Since then, I have seen Crohn's disease up close. The strength that is shown by Mike in his daily fight against this disease proves how strong he is and how strong his faith in God is. His writing of* Healthier than Normal *is a Christian act of the highest degree and a guiding light for all who have Crohn's or any illness."*

**Paul Twenge, head baseball coach, Valparaiso University**

*"God has placed Mike Florak right where He wants him: to show and share with people how to overcome adversity and challenges through faith.* Healthier than Normal *is another tool that can be used by everyone to gain inspiration to press on through tough times."*

**Pat Saunders, former area director, Fellowship of Christian Athletes**

# Table of Contents

# Chapter One

# Begging for a Miracle

# CHAPTER ONE — BEGGING FOR A MIRACLE

"I believe in miracles, I believe in miracles, I believe in miracles," I said again and again to myself as I lay weeping in the bathtub. I said this as I bargained with God for one more chance. I had been through some scary situations throughout my eight-year battle with the chronic intestinal condition known as Crohn's disease, but this one was the most desperate. It was early in the fall of 1996.

It was the eighth time in eight years that the disease flared up on me. Five teams of doctors from five different hospitals in the Midwestern United States had treated me during that time. All had recommended that I undergo a total colectomy, a surgical procedure to remove my entire colon and live the rest of my life with an ileostomy. Doctors told me that if I had the surgery, there was still a chance that the disease could manifest in my small intestine later on.

No one is really sure what causes Crohn's disease or its sister disease, ulcerative colitis. They are the two forms of Inflammatory Bowel Disease, and it is estimated that over two million people in the United States suffer from one of the two forms. There may be genetic and emotional contributors to the condition, but there is no certain cause or cure.

I had stubbornly refused doctors' prognostications that the disease, in my case, would not only become worse but also could lead to even more serious problems later. Nothing, not even a cancer scare, had been enough for me to consider this radical procedure.

It did not matter how often the disease came back in the form of these devastating flare-ups. It did not matter how much pain was endured by my body, my mind, my spirit, even my loved ones. I could not fathom having this procedure done.

The diagnosis was made shortly following the vicious onset of symptoms in 1989 when I was 22 years old. After that, I lived in fear that I would have to have the surgery, and I battled depression for a long time during the course of the illness. I vowed in all earnestness that I would take my own life before I would live with an ostomy. I never appreciated life much, and I appreciated it even less after I became ill.

I reaffirmed my vow to die every day. I knew what I would do–I would buy a gun. I knew the guy I would buy it from–a guy I went to school with when I was younger who had connections to get those things. I knew where I would do it–in the wooded area behind my parents' home, where no one could find me in time to save me in case I only wounded myself.

The struggle was as much psychological and spiritual as it was physical. I had been an athlete for most of my young life and thrived on being in control. I couldn't control, or even understand, this situation. Why had I prayed so hard for the disease to go away, yet it never did? Why had my family and friends and doctors tried to help me so much but it never mattered? What would the rest of my life be like? Would I ever be healthy or happy again? The answers to these questions always seemed to be "No."

I did most of the things the doctors said to do. I took all the medications, endured the painful, invasive tests, gritted my teeth and fought through the periodic flare-ups, and tried to keep surviving. Just when I thought I was making progress, the disease would wrap its ugly hands around my throat and choke away any hope I had.

During the eighth flare-up, reality was hitting home hard. The same symptoms had manifested again: severe fatigue, abdominal pain, diarrhea, nausea, perirectal abcesses, and bodily pain. Again as most of the others had, this flare-up was serious enough to leave me bedridden for several weeks preceding my admittance to the hospital.

Shortly after being admitted to Presbyterian University Hospital (PUH) in Pittsburgh, Pennsylvania, I was passing blood in my stool. This happened periodically throughout the course of the illness. This time, however, I was also severely dehydrated, compounded by the effects of losing some blood.

After three days of undergoing tests and being fed intravenously, the blood loss had been measured to the point where I had a better than ten percent chance of dying if I did not have a transfusion. I had the transfusion, albeit against my will, and temporarily dodged another bullet.

The next day was a new challenge. I had argued with several doctors, holding on strongly to the notion that only an emergency situation could make me consider having the surgery. On this day, my scrotum had filled with fluid that somehow drained in from my digestive tract and swelled to three times its normal size.

Urologists and colorectal surgeons were brought in. They agreed that my case was one that was most rarely seen. They again strongly suggested surgery, meanwhile prescribing powerful antibiotics and a high dose of steroids to decrease the inflammation. The surgeons also told me that there was a good chance (without having some type of surgical procedure to reroute the end of my digestive tract) that my genitals would become infected and possibly have to be removed.

I did not waver. Although I broke down emotionally, I stubbornly refused the surgery. I felt I could will myself to become well again. The doctors would monitor my progress as the second week of this hospital stay began. Part of me still wanted to die.

To the surprise of the doctors, the swelling began to decrease dramatically as the medication began to take effect. I had also continued my self-healing regimen, which I had learned over a period of time from various specialists in the health care field, including doctors, homeopaths, nurses, psychologists, massage therapists, dieticians, and nutritionists. All of these practices seemed to help the healing process, at least somewhat. However, human beings need to eat to live, and at that point, I had not eaten in six days.

On the seventh day I ate small meals, and everything seemed better but I was only fooling myself. While making arrangements for my discharge in a couple of days, the doctors warned me that I was making a horrible mistake.

I continued to eat the bland, torturous diet that I had been on for the previous five months. The diet had been prescribed by a nutritionist I had been seeing. I was permitted no dairy, red meats, bread, sugar, or foods that contained these products. This became extremely difficult, because much of the food in modern western society's diet contains one or more of these components. It was the latest in a long line of treatments and lifestyle adjustments I had made in effort to combat the disease.

Even this diet was not agreeable to a colon that was terribly diseased and inflamed. As I began eating again, although the abdominal pain and diarrhea were not as bad as usual, I just did not feel right as I anticipated being released the next day.

I made plans in the afternoon with my father to be picked up at the hospital after my discharge. We discussed my plan of action to treat the latest episode of the disease. The plan would include the special diet, which consisted of foods not well known and found only in small health stores. They would be hard for my parents to find. The plan would also include, of course, medication (a powerful combination of antibiotics, Flagyl and Cippro, and a high dose of an anti-inflammatory steroid called prednisone).

I would also use visualization techniques, plenty of rest, and hours upon hours of sitting in a hot bathtub. The bathtub had become my second home, or so it seemed. During flare-ups, I sat in water that was as hot as could humanly be tolerated to help drain the fluid from the perirectal abscesses. I would now try to use the same technique to help drain the fluid from my scrotal area through holes beneath my scrotum made by the surgeons a few days before.

After conversing with my father, I fell asleep. Hours later, I awoke to eat dinner, and I noticed some minor swelling in the scrotal area. I did not know what to expect. After going to the bathroom a couple times, the swelling became much worse.

At night, I had been requesting to be wheeled to another wing of the hospital that had a bathtub (there was no bathtub in the room in which I was staying). I called for the nurses to wheel me down to that area. I hoped that some time in the bathtub might help drain the swelling.

My mind was racing during this period. I knew that if I could not get the swelling to decrease that night, it would be a problem anytime I ate. My scrotum might fill with fluid and run the risk of infecting my testicles.

It was obvious that if the fluid would not drain, I would have to make a decision between my colon and my genitals. I was still saying to myself that I would rather be dead than live with an ostomy. I meant this with the utmost conviction.

As I filled the bathtub with water, I began to barter with God. All I wanted was a second chance (again). I write "again" because I lost count of how many times I had asked God for a second chance. I just wanted a sense of normalcy in my life that had been turned upside down eight years ago by this horrible disease.

Most 29-year-old men are not faced with having to choose between their colon, their genitals, or their life. I never asked, "Why me?" because the suffering I endured gave me a newfound perspective of suffering. I asked why people had to suffer at all. I did not merely wish to pass my short straw to someone else.

But this was my life. I was angry and bitter. Doing what I thought was the good Christian thing and accepting my suffering to strengthen myself evaded the realm of my behavior, but I still believed myself entitled to ask God for another second chance. Also, even more paradoxically, I told God that if I had to live with an ostomy, I would end my own life.

I struggled to get into the tub. I had i.v.'s in both arms that were covered with tape and couldn't touch the water without disrupting the flow of the tubes. I also had to be careful not to move suddenly from the i.v. pole, which was on wheels but weighed more than 50 pounds. If I moved away from the pole, the i.v. needle could come out of my arm and have to be restarted. This was one of the worst things about being hospitalized. The i.v.'s had left the veins in my arms mangled and misshapen.

The process of taking a bath in these conditions was rough. The i.v. pole was a huge concern, the tub was dirty, and my legs were weak from being sick for so long. It was hard to get in and out of the tub.

I had little control over my bowels. The bed sheets, the pad on the wheelchair seat, and the chair in the room were all soaked. Stool was leaking out into the bathtub as I watched in disgust.

The stool was coming out of my rectum. It was bad enough that I couldn't control my bowels, but it was also leaking from an incision that the surgeons had made between my testicles and rectum. Somehow, I thought this would all be worth it if I could get some of the fluid to drain out of my scrotum and into the tub.

As I sprawled out in the tub, I began to pray and meditate as I had done many times in the previous few years. Even though I was trying to hold God's will at gunpoint for what I wanted, I still had the audacity to ask God for a miracle. I knew that was what it would take in this situation. That's when I began begging, "I believe in miracles, I believe in miracles, I believe in miracles."

It is often said that "The Lord works in mysterious ways," and after having gone through this experience, I know it is true. In retrospect, a miracle did occur for me that night in the hospital. Being brought up

Catholic, I had believed in God all my life, but I had always thought I didn't receive the things I asked for because I was a bad person.

God, however, doesn't give us everything we ask for. I believe it is because God knows our needs better than we know ourselves. Now I understand that there was a plan for me and a method to all the madness for my suffering. The journey has not nearly ended, and it did not begin that night in the hospital or with the onset of the disease. It was a process that had begun with my birth nearly 30 years before.

14

# Chapter Two

# The Crystal Ball of the Past

## CHAPTER TWO — THE CRYSTAL BALL OF THE PAST

I was born in Pittsburgh, and my family moved to Steubenville, Ohio, when I was very young. My father was a college administrator, and my mother worked as a secretary for a prominent local businessman after my two younger brothers, Mark and Tim, and I were old enough to be in school during the day. My parents were loving, hard-working people with a zest for life and having fun.

The manner in which I grew up had a little bit to do with some aspects of the disease, like the onset, the suffering, the shame and guilt I felt about being weak and sick, and also the will to fight and endure the recovery process.

As I grew up, I was a shy, reticent kid. I remember that I had a sense that I didn't fit in with other kids, but I didn't know why. I was always scared in social situations. I would later learn that it was because I had a poor self-image. Small talk and making friends did not come easily for me. Withdrawing from people, especially my family, did come easily.

One thing that did help me overcome the painful shyness was sports. I was bigger than most of the kids my age, and as I grew older, it became increasingly apparent that I was blessed with a lot of athletic talent. I was competitive at an early age and would fight with my brothers and other kids over backyard games.

This attitude also helped fuel my withdrawing from people. I didn't get along very well with kids who didn't share my competitiveness. Adults reprimanded my fierce competitiveness. I became distrusting and somewhat rebellious.

During my adolescence, I continued to grow physically, and I was stronger than most kids my age. My surly disposition wasn't winning the affection of family or friends, but my athletic prowess was. I was turning into a big, mean athlete with a very high level of competitive desire, which were all great assets athletically, but not much personally. Sports were my outlet and in my distorted way of thinking, my only semblance of self-worth.

Around this time, I began to experiment with alcohol. During the early-to-mid 1980's, the success of the steel mills in eastern Ohio and western Pennsylvania was in decline, and alcohol and sports mixed

16

together sometimes to form an outlet for some frustrations of the economic situation of the region.

I attended Steubenville Catholic Central High School, and sports were a very important part of the school's identity. Our football team had a very long, proud tradition of being one of the toughest, hardest-hitting teams around, and playing with sportsmanship and class. We were well coached and disciplined.

By the time I was a junior, I had grown to 6'2" and over 200 pounds, and I ended up being a pretty good football player. We had good teams with tough kids who played hard and partied hard, too. I retained many of my friendships with those people for a long time.

My best sport, however, was baseball. I had good hand-eye coordination and the strength to swing a bat quickly and hit the ball a long way. I was left-handed, which gave me a distinct advantage when hitting mostly against right-handed pitchers. I also had a gift for understanding the game better than most of my peers. This understanding overlapped into other sports as I grew older.

The Steubenville American Legion baseball program is one of the best American Legion programs in the United States. Steubenville has won Ohio state championships in 1964, 1977, 1978, 1984, 1989, 1994, 1995, and 1998. A large number of the kids from those teams went on to earn scholarships to play Division I college baseball, and some were drafted by professional baseball teams. It is a first-class organization, and many great people have contributed much time and hard work to the program's success.

In 1983, I was fortunate enough to be selected to the team as a 16-year-old. It was quite an honor. I was one of the youngest of the 18 players chosen, and this represented the best baseball players from more than ten area high schools.

We would play over 60 games a summer. Forget about family vacations, or even a day at the beach. This was a serious commitment, and only those who truly loved baseball were involved.

The team's coaches were dedicated and genuinely concerned about the young men. Angelo "Ang" Vaccaro had stepped down as head coach before the 1983 season after nearly 40 years at the helm. He announced his retirement on opening day of the '83 legion season, at the dedication to the beautiful baseball complex that still bears his name on the University of Steubenville's campus.

Chuck Watt took over as head coach in my first season. He was an extremely knowledgeable, devoted man who loved baseball as much as any person I have ever known. He was a disciplined, tough-minded man who coached and pushed every one of his players to be better than his best. He and Tom "Red" Coulter were loyal coaches in the program for a very long time.

The person who meant the most to me in that program was Mark "Stacks" Stacy. He and John Maltese were younger coaches who were easy to relate to and took a special interest in the players who worked hard and responded to them.

Stacks and I developed a special relationship. He is blessed with a gift for being able to communicate to kids. He possesses as much baseball knowledge as one could ever hope to have. I ate up everything he had to offer. We would work and talk for hours on baseball fundamentals, especially hitting. He and one of my high school football coaches, Gregg Bahen, will always be two of the most influential people in my life.

Coach Bahen was a master motivator. He motivated with his intensity and pure love of athletics and young people. An ex-Marine, he was in his early-30's when I was in high school. He was in better physical condition than all of us. He still lifted weights and ran, and he could be a very intimidating presence with his crew cut, combat boots, and tattoos all over his big arms.

Coach Bahen loved to see hard work. He showed so much emotion, especially positive emotion, that you could not help but give 110 percent at every practice and game. He was my position coach in football, and I thrived on playing for him. My brother Mark was a quarterback on our teams, and we often quote Coach Bahen when we are together. That is how much Central football meant to most of us and still means to many of those who played.

I never worried about my health although I was really punishing myself. I was beginning to have trouble keeping my weight down, so I eliminated some meals. I sometimes drank too many beers on an empty stomach. We were young, tough, carefree, and, I thought, invincible.

Some days in the summer I would go to our football workouts at seven or eight in the morning, play a few games of playground basketball in the early afternoon, and then play in an American Legion baseball game at night. On the mornings of our varsity basketball games we would play street hockey in Holy Rosary gym. The league was organized by some of the guys in the class ahead of me, including John Buccigross, who would later become an anchor on ESPN. Many of the other guys I played with later found success in different areas of sports. Winning in all of those sports was almost a life or death proposition.

I personally continued to excel in athletics. I received interest from colleges for football, but it was becoming evident that I was certain to have a future in baseball. I did work harder than most of the kids I knew and the practice with Stacks and the other coaches was paying off. My dad would also work with me a lot.

Looking back, the most fun I ever had in sports were the times my dad would pitch whiffle balls to me in our backyard in preparation for my high-school and legion games. He would throw the balls hard, and using one of those skinny, yellow whiffle ball bats, or sometimes a broomstick honed my reflexes and hand-eye coordination. Sometimes these sessions would last almost an hour before it was time to go to the field for pregame practice.

My father gave a lot but wanted a lot out of me in return. He saw that I possessed talent and wanted me to make the most of it. Sometimes, I felt he was pushing too hard, and we would fight about it. I withdrew from my family even more although my dad continued to pitch to me and I kept improving as a player.

Academically, I underachieved. School was low on my list of priorities, and I clowned around in class a lot. I did that mostly to cover my insecurities. I finished high school with a 2.6 grade point average, which was well below what I was capable of. I underachieved socially, too. I was still very scared in social situations. I never spoke to new people unless I was spoken to first. I dated, but relationships with girls usually ended because of my insecurities or my wanting to party.

By my senior year, I received interest from a good number of schools for baseball. I accepted a scholarship to Ohio University in Athens, Ohio. We had played for the state American Legion championship on the school's campus. The coach, Jerry France, told me he needed a first baseman.

Coach France was a native of Steubenville and had played for Ang Vaccaro. He was a friendly, down-to-earth person who was known as a hard-nosed player in his day. He was great to me, and he was one of the reasons that I chose Ohio U. I wanted to major in communications, and the school had one of the country's finest programs. The campus is beautiful and very condensed for a large school. I was excited about the social life that OU offered.

My baseball skills seemed to be unaffected by my bad attitude and partying. My senior year of high school went great, and we made it all the way to the state semi-finals before losing. The week after the season ended, I received a great honor when I was selected by the Seattle Mariners in the 1985 amateur baseball draft.

Instead of it being one of the proudest moments of my life, deep down inside, I wished it wouldn't have happened. I had begun to put a lot of pressure on myself. I felt I had to be perfect every time I stepped on the field. My lack of self-esteem made a large part of me feel undeserving. It seemed like another reason that I just didn't fit in with the "normal" kids I was growing up with.

The economic and social climate in Steubenville was not good at the time. The situation with the steel mill industry, which was the staple of the job market, was becoming more bleak. Many people, including some of my friends' fathers, were laid off. Any positive event was celebrated and welcomed with wide-open arms. My being drafted was one of the events I was fortunate enough to celebrate.

In 1984, I was a part of the Steubenville American Legion baseball team that won the state championship. Our archrival, Steubenville High School, also won the state football championship that year. The area had local sports going well, and those teams evoked a great deal of pride for the residents.

People treated the kids on those teams as though we were very special. At the time, there were few kids from the area who were doing well in sports at higher levels. I was the first baseball player drafted out of Steubenville in a while, but there was still a wait-and-see type of attitude about how I would fare after I left the area. I'm not sure anyone knew what to expect.

I decided to pass up the contract that Seattle offered me. It was worth probably only a year's tuition at Ohio U. That wasn't the reason that I didn't go. I just didn't think I was good enough. I was totally naïve about the whole situation and merely happy to be playing a college sport.

I thought sports were what gave me an identity, and that baseball would give me a few more years to feel like I was worth something. I simply didn't understand at the time that being a good athlete wasn't what made one a good person. Every time I was introduced to someone, it was, "Oh yeah, you played football for Central," or "You're the baseball player." It was never, "I heard you're a good guy," because I wasn't. I thought I didn't have to be because people would treat me better than others because of my success in sports. I had no real relationships with anyone, including my family. I still knew they loved and supported me, though. I never had to give anything. All I had to do was keep receiving pats on the back and play well and party hard.

As adults, we often gaze into the crystal ball of our past. The way we would do things all over again always appears to be perfectly clear in that crystal ball. Time cannot be turned back, though. The decisions we make as adults seem easier when peer pressure, raging hormones, immaturity, and teenage angst are not factors. Obviously, I made bad decisions that I would like to take back, especially my general attitude about what was important in life.

I remember a letter Coach Bahen wrote to me before we played Steubenville High School in football during my senior year. The coaches did this for all the seniors as part of the tradition of preparing for the big city championship game. In the letter, Coach Bahen wrote about "keeping my priorities straight and a bright future lay ahead." That was a covert way of telling me not to party my way out of my athletic career. It didn't really register with me at the time.

# Chapter Three

# A Profound Impact

## CHAPTER 3 — A PROFOUND IMPACT

I thought college would be different for me at first. I was a bit nervous about leaving home, but Athens is less than a three-hour drive from Steubenville. If I became homesick, it would not be hard to find a ride home if I had time to go.

Academically, I lacked confidence because of my track record. I was a marginal student mainly because of my lack of enthusiasm toward studying, but I had a good attendance record. I attended every class session of my math class. At the end of the quarter, the professor, Charles Wilson, gave me an extra ten points for being there every day.

The ten extra points gave me a C+ for a grade. It may not seem like much, but I was proud of it because I had failed senior math in high school. The amazing part was that I made it to class every morning, Monday through Friday, beginning at 8 a.m. for ten weeks, and I sat and listened. I was enjoying the freedom and the college social life.

College was a whole new opportunity for me to develop my social skills. A good friend of mine, Ronnie DeLuca, started taking graduate classes at Ohio U. in the fall of '85. He worked part-time as a bartender on one of the bars on Court Street. He was the older brother of one of my good friends, Danny DeLuca. I practically grew up in their house. They lived up the street from my parents, and I spent as much time at their place as I did ours. Danny and I and our friends often hung out in their basement. I began spending too much time in Ronnie's bar and the rest of the places on Court Street.

My classes went okay that first quarter, and I worked very hard to keep the grades up. My only real motivation to do this, however, was to stay eligible for baseball. The fall practice season went much better than I expected.

I started out in the intrasquad scrimmages slowly. Coach France remained patient with me, however, and didn't change anything in my swing. He kept encouraging me. After a few weeks, I was starting to hit the ball to all fields with extra-base power and consistency.

Defensively, I continued to improve. During my last year of legion ball, I had made the adjustment to playing first base. I had played outfield most of my life before that year. Most people involved in baseball will agree that the transition from outfield to infield is much tougher than the other way around. When I was 17 years old, I struggled at first base. Stacks and Coach Watt stuck with me and, at the same time, worked me to death. I took those habits to college, and I would take 50-75 extra ground balls per day. I had made myself into a very good defensive first baseman.

When our fall season wrapped up, I didn't want it to end because I was hitting the ball so well. I was finally learning to hit the ball to left field for power. Although I wasn't fast, my savvy made me an excellent baserunner. I had won the starting first baseman's job. There was a question of how well I would handle the best pitching that other teams had to offer when the regular season began in the spring. Our staff was young and not very deep, so my success in the fall would not be a good barometer as far as my potential to succeed as a hitter. As fall semester ended, I was anxious for the season to come.

Ohio University's quarter system allows for classes to be recessed from the week of Thanksgiving until after New Year's Day. I worked at the post office during our break as a Christmas casual. I lifted weights a little. I partied way too much.

Danny DeLuca went to West Liberty State College, along with a few of our other good friends, Maz Zyinyi, Matt Morrison, Paul Walkosky, and Pat Lanaghan. There were weeknight parties on the campus, which was only 40 minutes from Steubenville. It was an easy drive to have a place to party for a night. When we weren't up there, we would tour the bars in Steubenville.

During this period, I continued to drift farther and farther away from my family. I don't recall many conversations that lasted more than a minute with either of my parents. I slept and ate at home, and that was basically it. I would sleep late every day, maybe work out at the gym, and be at work at the post office at four o'clock. Then I would hang out with friends or go out on the town.

Nothing else had any value to me, just baseball and partying, and not necessarily in that order. My grades would fall the next semester. I was losing sight of my priorities. I stopped going to church. I didn't appreciate my family, or even my friends for that matter. In general, my attitude was lousy.

When January rolled around, baseball practice began again. My skills continued to improve. If my attitude had been better and I had more confidence in myself, I would have been even better than I was. What I wanted more than anything was to be accepted by family and peers and to be normal, to fit in with everyone.

God had blessed me with a talent that was not normal, though. I began launching baseballs into the trees and onto the Grover Center sundeck that were behind the outfield fence at Ohio U.'s Trautwein Field during batting practice. I was gifted with instincts for baseball that were exceptional. I could see things on the field before they would happen. I picked up fundamentals and techniques quickly. Things just clicked in my mind.

When I had just turned seven years old, I watched the Rose Bowl on New Year's Day at my father's uncle's house. I can remember that Lynn Swann was the best player on the field that day. I hoped that my favorite football team, the Pittsburgh Steelers, would draft him. Swann was the Steelers' first-round pick that year and was a star on all four Super Bowl winning teams. He was elected to the Pro Football Hall of Fame. It was amazing that at such a young age I could understand these things. This was something I was truly gifted with. These instincts were present for me in most sports I played.

I honed these instincts throughout my baseball career. Many times, I could pick up a little idiosyncrasy, a twitch, or a movement by a pitcher that would tell me what pitch was coming. It was the same thing in high-school football. Often, I could tell by looking at opponents' stances or formations which direction a play was going. Although I foolishly never learned to fully trust these instincts, sometimes I did permit them to give me a big advantage.

In college, I got into weightlifting a little more than I had in high school. This helped me with my swing. My arms became strong and that gave me another advantage.

I parlayed my physical tools, the instincts, and the great coaching I received into a very good freshman season. I started nearly every game, and I hit well over .300 with about 45 percent of my hits being for extra bases (the major league average was about 30 percent at the time). I played great defense. Tony Lucadello, the longtime Philadelphia Phillies scout who signed hall of famer Mike Schmidt, called me a very good prospect.

At home that summer, I continued to party hard. The old gang was together again. The boys were back in town. We were finally old enough

26

at age 19 to drink legally. We frequented a place called "Angelo's" that was conveniently located about a mile from my parents' home.

I had a couple of grass cutting jobs, and I worked as a lifeguard at a local pool for a while. I was also playing baseball in a semi-pro league in the area. On that team were several of my old teammates from our '84 glory days: Matt Morrison, Joe Pierro, Mike Nodianos, Rick Grimm, and other guys from teams we competed against. It was a lot of fun but not a great league for a serious college player to test his skills. Testing my skills wasn't top priority for me, though.

Although baseball was giving me the attention I always desired, I had ambivalent feelings about it. People bought me drinks and asked how I was doing. I always tried to deflect the attention. I didn't want people to think that I was a one-dimensional person, even though baseball was one of the few things that could capture my attention. I was confused and very immature about the things that I wanted.

I was having so much fun, or so I thought. Everyone kept telling me what a great future I had, but I couldn't see that then because I had no self-confidence. I had everything a 19-year-old could want. The stupid decisions I made every day would have a profound impact on the rest of my life.

# Chapter Four

# No More Denying It

# CHAPTER FOUR — NO MORE DENYING IT

My freshman year at college, I was pretty much a loner. I hadn't made friends too quickly in high school but this was worse. With the large university being on such a small campus, I saw many of the same people every day, but I was shy about making new friends. That changed in my sophomore year.

I moved to another side of campus, closer to the baseball field and our other practice facilities. Many other athletes lived on that side of campus. At first, I liked the old side better. I was inconspicuous and I had privacy. On this side, everyone knew each other, and there were plenty of parties to attend.

I felt that physically I needed alcohol to relax. It helped bring out some of the emotions that I had suppressed for so long, even though many were negative. Baseball was the only other thing I could become excited about. I had psychologically convinced myself that I needed to drink to be comfortable in social situations. I worshipped the partying lifestyle as though it were a religion.

This was indicative of where my spiritual life was at the time. I had no relationship with God. I had no relationship with anyone, really. I didn't even care about myself. My low self-esteem would not allow me to think about myself unless it was negative. Alcohol and athletics gave me a false sense of well-being. As long as I had those two things in my life, I felt worthy of existence on earth.

The next couple years went by in the blink of an eye. My athletic career would not improve on its strong beginning.

In the beginning of my sophomore season, I decided to try to pull the ball more. I changed my hitting style to do so. Many scouts believe (and erroneously so) that to have true power, a hitter has to pull the ball down the foul lines. The distance for a home run is shorter down the lines than it is to the gaps and center field. I had learned to use the whole field when I was 17, but three years later, I decided to go back to being a one-dimensional hitter. I did hit more homeruns that year than I had ever hit before, but my batting average dropped about 60 points and I struck out more. I developed a terrible overswing. The homeruns were nice but I was not a good hitter overall. I just wanted to please the scouts.

I should have just tried to progress as I was. My lack of confidence and self-esteem played a large role in my decision to change my swing. Nothing I ever did was good enough for me, in baseball or in life. I was terminally unhappy.

The next two years, my performance was average at best. The stats were okay, but I was still much better when I was a freshman. After my sophomore and junior seasons, I failed miserably in two summer league seasons, one in the Valley League in Virginia and one in the Great Lakes league for a team in Columbus, Ohio. These were two of the best college leagues in the country. They were supposed to be measuring sticks for pro prospects. In hindsight, I was more than good enough. I should have done well in those leagues but I didn't. I didn't have enough confidence to succeed.

I was starting to feel apathetic toward baseball. Physically, I was feeling wiped out. My diet was poor, and I began having unusual sleeping patterns during my sophomore year. I would sleep for three hours at night, then need a two-hour nap during the day. It didn't help that I had also become addicted to smokeless tobacco, which can contribute to the disturbance of sleep patterns because of its high nicotine content. It can also affect one's digestive tract.

I had also developed unusual habits as far as other bodily functions. Several bowel movements per day were becoming the norm, and I began experiencing abdominal discomfort. I remember our catcher, Ralph Dillman, kidding me about eating greasy, fast food that we always bought on our road trips. He was my roommate on the road, and we were always getting on each other about something. You become like brothers during the course of a college baseball season because you spend so much time sweating, bleeding, eating, talking, and doing everything else together.

After one road trip to Ball State University, my insides were burning. It was the middle of my junior year. I was off to a good start, hitting around .400 with good power. On that trip, I felt worse than usual after a large fast food meal. Ralph and I joked about how many times I went to the bathroom, and I really thought little of it at the time. I was young and indestructible. A physical problem was out of the question, in my mind.

I had never missed an athletic contest in my life because of injury. I thought all physical maladies were for people who were too weak to overcome them. I attributed the change in my bowel habits to my drinking, chewing tobacco, poor diet, or anything but a physical condition that would mean I was "weak."

In college, I continued to develop an attitude that I was really "tough." Not tough in the sense that I would beat people up, but in the sense that nothing could bring me down. I treated my body "tough" also. I didn't get enough rest and I slept and ate poorly. These would prove to be lethal habits when combined with the use of tobacco products and alcohol to embarrassing excess. I had a poor self-image to go along with all the other problems. My body, mind, and soul were ripe for a major overhaul.

I spent the summer preceding my senior year playing in the Great Lakes Collegiate League for the Columbus (Ohio) All-Americans. Ralph, Dave Adams (another Ohio U. teammate), and I played for Joe Carbone, who was formerly an assistant coach at Ohio State. Shortly before that summer season began, Joe was named to replace Coach France at Ohio U. for what would be my senior year.

Joe was a hard-driving, all business, type-A personality who was going to turn things upside down. Ralph, Dave and I learned that quickly in the summer. I performed poorly and found myself on the bench.

I didn't think much of it then, but now I remember having to take extra trips to the outhouse at our home field at Hilliard High School. I was also growing weaker physically.

Team members were given a pass to lift at an area gym. I would lift there with Paul DiBiase, a good friend of mine from high school. We had played football together, and he was my lifting partner. He was doing an internship at Ohio State's medical school.

Paul was playing football at Harvard. He was a good person to lift with because he worked hard, and he would push me to do the same. Paul recognized that I had become weaker than I was in high school. We would joke that the difference between playing baseball and football in college was that football players got stronger and baseball players got fatter. In all seriousness, I didn't understand my sudden loss of strength. Although this should have been another warning sign that something was wrong with me, I shrugged it off, too.

I began to hit the ball a little better toward the end of that summer season. Coach Carbone worked with me a lot. He is known across the country as one of college baseball's finest teachers, and it started to pay off for me. I thought I might get back on track for my senior year. I had a good fall season.

As the start of the spring regular season was approaching, Coach Carbone and I started to butt heads. He has always been very demanding of his players and my bad attitude was primed for an adjustment.

Even though I was hitting the ball better, I had little power. I had to pull the ball almost straight down the right field line to hit a home run. That hadn't been the case since I was 15 years old.

Still, none of these occurrences made me stop to think that something might be wrong. In the back of my mind, perhaps, but the young "toughman" always won out mentally. I was killing myself with my rotten lifestyle and priorities, and all the other bad things I was doing for myself.

Mentally, I was a wreck. It was becoming obvious that I would not have another chance to play professional baseball. There was a part of me that was still the innocent little kid who cried when it became too dark to play because it meant that he would have to wait until his father came home from work the next day to play again. That is how much a part of me loved baseball.

The part of me that was stronger, though, was the one that told myself again and again that kids from Steubenville don't make it in athletics. It was the same part that told me I would be a laughing stock if I chased a dream that was so unfathomable for so many people. It was that part of me that just wanted to fit in.

My attitude became worse. I was beginning to feel worthless. I believed that without having an identity as a baseball player, my life wasn't worth living. I withdrew even from the friends who thought they were closest to me. I felt as though I was the least happy person on earth. It may not have seemed that way because I was still partying, but even the partying was not as much fun as it used to be.

One of my friends used to joke that drinking seemed like a chore on certain nights. That is what it had become to me. Everything seemed like a chore. The only social dialogue I had with anyone was during the course of night of partying. My interests were limited. I was a mundane, sad person. I didn't really care about anything. I was only existing and not really living.

We had a very good season during my senior season in 1989. We were in contention for the Mid-American Conference title right up until Western Michigan nosed us out on the last weekend. Coach Carbone re-energized a once-proud program that had become stagnant. He was an alumnus, and he and our assistant coach, Bill Toadvine, had played on the 1970 Ohio U. team that made it to the College World Series. They made my senior year fun because we became winners.

I was given the Bob Wren Run-Maker Award, which Coach Carbone instituted to give to the player who produced the most runs offensively for the team. It was named after the late legend who coached at Ohio U. from 1949-72. My stats were not great, but I hit a few key home runs that helped us win important conference games. I was disappointed in myself personally, as usual. We won most of our games because we had great pitching and played great defense.

After the season ended, I began bartending at one of the bars on Court Street that I used to hang out at called the "C.I." I thought this would be my future. Some of my friends were doing the same thing in other college towns, and the money was okay for a college student. Besides, I spent so much time in those places, why not get paid to do it?

I had a bitter taste in my mouth from baseball. Although the way Coach Carbone had turned us around enabled me to end my career on a good note, I was still disappointed, even ashamed, of the way I had performed. Baseball wasn't fun for me anymore but that was my own fault. Despite the amount of effort I put in and the love I had for the sport for so long, I harbored only ambivalent feelings toward baseball.

Strangely, a couple of teams were still interested in me. I had calls for some tryouts. No contract offers, but chances nonetheless. The tryouts would go on throughout the summer, and I was keeping myself in shape, doing some lifting and some hitting when I wasn't working and taking summer classes.

One tryout I was supposed to attend in late June was cancelled because of rain. It was rescheduled for mid-July, and there were a few others at that time. I was anticipating them but not with the eagerness that I should have had. Something was wrong. I continued to get physically weaker, although I was lifting and working at the bar more and drinking less. I slept more. I became moodier. Something was wrong with me physically but I could not face the truth. With the events that transpired on July 7, 1989, there was no more denying it.

# Chapter Five

# The Nightmare Begins

## CHAPTER FIVE — THE NIGHTMARE BEGINS

I had been out all night the night before. When I awoke on July 7, I felt a terrible pain in the left side of my abdomen. I ran to the bathroom with watery diarrhea.

It wasn't the first time I had had diarrhea after a hard night of drinking. It wasn't the first time I had experienced abdominal pain, either. This time was different, though. A half-hour later, I had to go again. This time, when I got off the toilet, I looked down to see blood everywhere. The pain in my side was getting worse.

The whole day continued that way. Five, eight, ten, up to 15 bloody stools. I thought maybe I had eaten something that was bad or that I just got carried away with the drinking the night before. I melted into the couch all day and stayed close to the bathroom until it was time to go to bed.

I ate nothing that day. It was not uncommon for me to go a whole day without eating while I was in college, or even in high school. I always saved food money to use for beer.

To this point, my desire to drink had affected my need for relationships with family and friends, my desire to study and play baseball, and even to perform necessary, normal human functions like sleeping and eating. Now I was really bummed out and sick, and July 8 was much of the same.

After my tenth trip to the bathroom that day, I was feeling totally wiped out. The pain increased to the point that it felt like someone was jabbing a red-hot poker into my side. I had a fever and I was feeling thirsty, which was a sign of dehydration. I called a cab to take me to O'Bleness Memorial Hospital, which was on the outskirts of Athens. It was ten minutes away from the house in which I was living.

I staggered to the cab. I tried to deflect attention from myself as usual, but the cabbie could see the pain I was in.

"What the hell is wrong with you, buddy?" he asked.

I just groaned. He repeated the question, this time with a little more urgency.

"I've been shitting blood for two days," I snapped back at him. "Just take me to O'Bleness."

In O'Bleness, I explained my symptoms to the nurse on duty. It was late at night so the hospital was nearly empty. She said that the doctor on duty would be in to see me shortly, and, to my surprise, he was. After a few questions, he told me to get undressed to prepare for a sigmoidoscopy.

I had never even heard of a sigmoidoscopy, nor was I able to spell or pronounce it. I soon found out that it was a long, thin tube with a scope on the end of it that is inserted into the rectum and used to look into the sigmoid colon, which is in the lower left quadrant of the organ. I also found out that it was painful.

Maybe this is a bad case of food poisoning, I thought. I was hoping for a quick diagnosis and some antibiotics. The doctor that was on duty was only a general practitioner and wasn't really qualified to determine what the problem really was.

"I'd like to refer you to a specialist in a larger hospital," the doctor said. "There is a lot of inflammation in your sigmoid colon, and I'm not really sure what it is from."

I got dressed and called for another cab. All this trouble for food poisoning, I thought. I went back into the house, and spent the night continuing almost hourly trips to the bathroom.

I called my mother the next day and told her what was happening. She was alarmed, much more than I was. Of course, when a loved one reports ill feelings, even in my case as a relatively heathly 22-year-old, one is naturally concerned. Blood coming out of internal organs could heighten the fear. For my mother, it had the potential for déjà vu.

About four years earlier, her father, John Bartell, had been diagnosed with colon cancer. His first symptoms included rectal bleeding. Fortunately, his cancer was diagnosed early and surgery saved his life. He was very sick for a while, and he struggled at first with having to live with a colostomy.

My mother was right by his side the whole way. She is the most compassionate, thoughtful person I know, and she gets very emotionally involved whenever she sees anyone who needs help. It was ironic that I now needed her because my relationship with my parents had deteriorated because of my withdrawing and wild ways.

She was disappointed in my behavior, and she had let me know about it. I saw this as a threat to my ego and internalized her constructive criticism. I stopped communicating with her except when it came to superficial needs. I always had a deep understanding, though, that if I ever really needed anything, my parents would do anything in their power to help.

After my dad picked me up and took me back to Steubenville, they drove me to Allegheny General Hospital in Pittsburgh, which was only one hour away. There I could have the tests performed that could result in a diagnosis and proper treatment.

The first couple days I was in Allegheny General, I started to feel a little bit better. The hospital's gastroenterological team prescribed antibiotics for what they thought was a severe case of food poisoning. I didn't eat any food during those first few days, and the diarrhea subsided.

I had lost some weight, maybe about ten to 15 pounds, but I was still above 200. I think that may have been one reason that the doctors were not too concerned. At least I still looked good. They told me to wait another day before I began eating. It was my fifth day in the hospital. I started to think about going to the Who concert that was coming up in a few weeks at Three Rivers Stadium. The consensus was that I would be back on my feet in no time.

On the sixth day, I ate solid food for the first time. The breakfast and lunch went okay. My abdominal discomfort hadn't returned, and I packed the clothes my mother brought for me into a gym bag. I couldn't wait to get out.

After dinner that night, I drank a big vanilla milkshake. Almost immediately afterward, the bloody stools and the abdominal pain returned with a vengeance. I couldn't believe it! I knew then that this was more than a case of food poisoning, and it wasn't just a reaction to the milkshake, either.

The nurse on duty paged a doctor. When the doctor saw me later that evening, he told me he was recommending that I be kept another day so the gastro team could review my case. I called and told my parents the news so they wouldn't have to come early in the morning to pick me up.

The symptoms were the same. I felt feverish, and I was going to the bathroom about every two hours. The sharp sting in my left side was relieved only by going to the bathroom. I was starting to worry that I had something wrong with me that I might never get over.

When they examined me the next morning, the doctors told me not to eat anything. They were going to do a biopsy and a sigmoid colonoscopy the following day. There had to be as little activity in my digestive system as possible. The thought that I might have cancer never occurred to me until I heard the word "biopsy." It was a possibility, especially considering the family history. My father's uncle had died from colon cancer.

38

A severe case of food poisoning was still not out of the question. I knew several people who had experienced bad cases of food poisoning in which the symptoms lasted for a couple weeks before they recovered. Also, for the first time, the doctors began mentioning the possibility that I had a form of inflammatory bowel disease (IBD). It was a term I had heard before because I knew a few people who had ulcerative colitis and Crohn's disease, which are the two forms of IBD. I was still holding out my hopes for the food poisoning scenario.

After a couple of painful days of diarrhea, nausea, vomiting, and worry, the doctors had the results of the biopsy. There was no sign of cancer, which is usually a cause for thankfulness and optimism. The doctors were not happy to report, however, that there was a lot of inflammation in my sigmoid colon and that I had what looked to be a case of ulcerative colitis.

It was not what I wanted to hear, but I didn't think it would be a big deal. The people I had known with ulcerative colitis all experienced one major attack, were hospitalized, watched their diets for a while, then returned back to normal. I figured the same would happen to me.

The doctors prescribed Sulfasalazine, an anti-inflammatory drug that was standard protocol for fighting IBD. I also started to eat very lightly again, but the symptoms persisted.

After several more days, I still showed no improvement. The doctors ordered me to stop eating to give my digestive system a rest. My weight was down to about 190, a loss of nearly 30 pounds. After a little more than two weeks of hospitalization, the doctors told me I had two options, surgery or steroids.

For the first time, I became scared. They explained the surgical possibilities. I might have to have only part of my colon removed and have the two other ends rejoined. The other possibility was that I would have to have a larger portion of my colon removed and would have to have a colostomy. I was sad and disgusted.

I had become very vain in the couple years preceding the illness. My body mattered more to me than many things. I looked good at 220 pounds, and people always remarked at my muscularity or what a strong handshake I had. My body, my physicality, was my identity. I think sometimes I pushed my body so hard on the outside because I didn't like the person on the inside. The thought of having my body disfigured by any surgery, especially for an ostomy, was absolutely out of the question. I chose the steroids.

Prednisone is the steroid that is prescribed for many inflammatory conditions such as IBD. Prednisone's purpose is the opposite of anabolic steroids that are taken by athletes and bodybuilders—that is, to shrink, not enlarge tissue. It is powerful and mostly effective. It is often the last medical option for patients whose IBD has not responded to other therapies.

The problem with prednisone, however, is that it possesses all the same side effects as anabolic steroids. These side effects include, but are not limited to, rapid weight gain, acne, bloating of the face and hands, cataracts, joint pain, skin rashes, increased appetite, mood swings, and depression. Doctors are often hesitant to prescribe prednisone because it is an easy drug to become dependent on, and the side effects can last for a long time after the course of the prescribed use or even become permanent.

The gastro team at Allegheny General was very cautious with its use of prednisone. In fact, I got the sense that they almost feared putting me on the drug. They also freely admitted to me that they did not know all that much about IBD. In the late 1980's, the whole medical profession was just starting to learn more about digestive disorders, especially at certain hospitals that devoted time and concern to those areas. Unfortunately, Allegheny General was not one of those hospitals. It was the hospital that my family had gone to and received successful treatment for other illnesses. We believed at the time it would be the best place for me to get attention for what seemed to be an acute situation.

The doctors started me on a conservative dose of 40 milligrams of prednisone. It was taken intravenously with other supplements that were fed through the i.v. tube in one arm or the other since the first day I was admitted. Those supplements helped stabilize the minerals, vitamins, and fluids that were being depleted by the disease. It was expected that within a 48-72 hour period, I would feel substantial improvement.

That improvement never came. The abdominal pain and other symptoms continued after 72 hours. The doctors said this was unexpected but that some patients did struggle this much with the disease. The doctors reluctantly decided to increase the dose of prednisone to 100 milligrams per day. I also had to have a large i.v. inserted beneath my clavicle to get as many nutrients as possible into larger arteries. It was too much for the smaller veins in my arms to take.

These i.v.'s, both in the arms and under the clavicle, caused a great deal of pain upon insertion. Fortunately, I have a high threshold of pain. Really, anyone with inflammatory bowel disease must have a high tolerance for physical discomfort. It was not that I am unusually brave or tough. The technician who inserted the i.v. under my clavicle remarked that she had never seen a patient who was so stoic. I figured I shouldn't make other people miserable just because I was, especially the people who were trying to help me.

The way I treated my family was a different story. I was surly and flat-out mean to my parents. A priest who would later counsel me told me that it was just the disease talking. Many times when people are sick, unhappy, and depressed, they take out their feelings on those closest to them. At that time, I was in physical pain, but I was also frustrated by the end of my baseball career.

My mother drove an hour every day to the hospital just to visit me. My father left work early many times just to make sure I was okay. I felt guilty about this. I failed to understand that they wanted to do this out of love for their child. With my self-loathing being compounded by the physical pain I was in, I tried to drive them away.

"Mom, I feel bad about you having to be here all the time," I would say.

"I want to be here for you, though," she would reply.

It made me feel bad that I was interrupting their lives. I figured by this stage in my life, I would be totally independent. I didn't think I would need anyone, especially my parents, to take care of me.

The lack of progress kept frustrating me. I was scared that I would have to have surgery. I began to doubt whether I had colitis. I argued with my father about it. It was my insecure way of trying to obtain reassurance. They would ask me how I felt and I would explode on them.

"How the hell do you think I feel?" I would shout. "I'm in constant pain and I can't stop going to the bathroom. The medication is driving me up a f—ing wall, and it is not working! I don't think the doctors know what is really wrong with me!"

"Well, just what do you think is wrong with you?" my father would ask. It was almost like old times when we used to fight over my hitting techniques during baseball season.

"I don't know what is wrong with me," I would yell back. "But it is not what they are saying it is."

The doctors became puzzled by my lack of progress. The doctors even brought up AIDS as a possibility. In 1989, it was almost unheard of for heterosexuals to be diagnosed with AIDS, but my doctors were considering it. The situation was a cause for growing concern but fortunately, blood tests for AIDS proved to be negative. It was some form of IBD.

Finally, after almost 25 days in the hospital, I started to turn the corner. The diarrhea decreased and so did the pain in my abdomen. The high dose of steroids finally kicked in, and the doctors warned that I would have to be taken off them quickly. They would keep me on a high dose for the 26th day, then take me down to 60 milligrams per day, then three days later down to 40, and permit me to ingest food again.

I had gone an incredible 15 days without food, and seven of them without a drop of water. I was fed only through the i.v. that was sticking out beneath my clavicle. I could see the pain on the faces of my family and friends when they visited me. I tried to act brave and make jokes, but I knew with my newly frail body and wires sticking out of my neck, I wasn't a pretty sight. The doctors thought that the best way to let my colon heal was to give it total rest, although the time frame had to be expanded to 15 days because my recovery was so slow.

The lack of food and activity had caused my weight to drop to 170 pounds. Most of the time, the abdominal pain was so fierce that I couldn't get out of bed unless it was to stagger to the bathroom. Friends and relatives would call and ask if I was getting up and moving, but it was hard to get up because the pain was so great. It was much more than the average bellyache.

My fluctuating energy level was hard to understand. Steroids are very deceiving. They made me feel as if I were on top of the world one minute and the next, I was so angry that I wanted to spit in the face of the person across from me. They also left me wired and unable to sleep. It denied me not only physical rest but also the mental rest that was needed so I could have six or seven hours a day to take my mind off being sick.

As much as I had detached myself from caring about anything or anyone, there was no denying that people cared for me. I had many visitors. Most of my old friends from high school came up several times. My friends from Ohio U. stopped by, including Mark "Frog" Mihalyo, Dave Gaertner, and John Mascaro. We would talk about what we were going to do next year because most of us still had classes to take before we graduated. By all indications, I was going to have a normal future.

On about the 30th day of my stay, I began to eat small portions. God, did that hospital breakfast taste good! Fifteen days without eating had left me with a newfound appreciation for food. Eating is an incredible gift that God gives to us that we sometimes take for granted. During those first few bites, all of the pain and suffering I had endured over the past month almost seemed worth it for the pleasure of plain scrambled eggs.

For the next couple days, I continued to eat and feel better on 40 milligrams of steroids per day. I was going to the bathroom about three times daily, and the doctors were concerned about this. I told them that this had been normal for me for several years, and they finally relented.

After 35 days, I was discharged. I was terribly weak. I had lost 50 pounds, which the doctors said was common for someone my size who had gone through a bout with IBD. At the time of my release, I was still on 40 milligrams of prednisone per day, which the doctors ordered to be tapered down ten milligrams per week until I was off the drug completely. I thought to myself that this would be the first time that I could eat like a pig and not have to worry about being too fat to field a ground ball.

My body had been through so much turmoil that I could not walk all the way from my room in the hospital to the car in the parking lot without stopping to rest a couple of times. When that happened, I realized that I had a long way to go before I was well again.

# Chapter Six

# Not a Car

## CHAPTER SIX — NOT A CAR

The first couple of days that I was home, I slept a lot. It is hard to get much sleep in the hospital. Every couple hours, you're being tested for something. The surroundings are foreign and uncomfortable. Prednisone can also cause night sweating, along with general discomfort. It was the first time I could remember just sleeping in at home for three straight days without rushing off to practice or to party.

My mother is an excellent cook. She prepared some awesome five-course meals for me. The prednisone had made my appetite three times what it normally was. I gained a couple pounds the first week, up to about 172. The doctors said it would be another month before I should exercise and that I should take some time to rest. I would walk about a half-mile up the street during the first few days, just trying to get some strength back.

The second week at home was much of the same. I gained a couple more pounds, and a lot of people were coming by the house to wish me well. I worked my way up to walking one mile per day, and I was starting to feel a little better.

When the third week began, I reduced the prednisone to 20 milligrams per day, as the doctors ordered. Something happened almost immediately that alarmed me very much. I started to use the bathroom a lot that very day.

I wasn't really having any pain, but having six bowel movements per day is not normal for anyone, not even someone with IBD. I knew that this was a bad sign, and I made an appointment to see the doctors the next day. They still insisted that I reduce the dose of steroids to ten milligrams per day in another week. They were concerned about the negative turn that my recovery had taken and made another appointment for me to come back the following week.

When I reduced the prednisone at the start of the next week, the bloody stools returned. I also had ulcers in my mouth and throat, making it painful to swallow. It became hard to eat. I saw the doctors at Allegheny General, and they advised me that they had done all they could do for me and told me to go to a larger hospital with a more advanced treatment of IBD. They also told me that I could continue my treatment there, but they suggested that I have my colon removed soon.

My parents and I were floored. It is such a helpless, low feeling when doctors tell you that they have done all they can do for you. In modern Western society, we place so much credence in the opinions of medical doctors, sometimes elevating them to almost deity-like status. When they give you bad news about your health, it is almost as if the hand of God has struck you down. I felt like I was in a state of shock.

It seemed like I was an entirely different person from the one who had finished a fairly accomplished athletic career just a few short months ago. I was much different, also, from the one who loved the reckless nightlife and cared little for the world, outside of what felt good to me.

The teams of doctors in Athens and Pittsburgh knew very little about inflammatory bowel disease, and my parents and I knew even less. We decided that I should continue my treatment at the Cleveland Clinic. I would have to delay my return to school and worry about finishing my degree later. My health was now by far my number one concern. The condition and the symptoms had dominated my life for almost three months.

I was having more abdominal pain and going to the bathroom about ten times per day. I was also very fatigued, and my weight had dropped to 160 pounds, down from 220. I looked even worse than this sounds. My parents were beginning to panic. I was numbed by the metamorphosis I was going through. I didn't understand why this was happening. I would ask, plead, and pray for help when I wasn't cursing God.

Many people who endure suffering or hardships ask God for help at one time or another. In my time of hardship it was hard for me to realize what I would later come to know—that God has a plan for all of us. I didn't trust in those plans enough. I had no idea at the time that God was leading me down a path that had a long way to go.

Despite the suffering that we endure sometimes, there are rays of hope, bright spots that are sent into our lives when we need them. I would later come to believe that these people and occurrences happen for a reason. I had always fought things in my life, and I tried to overcome things instead of learning that I should trust God and follow the plan. The rays of hope are sent to help us persevere through the tough times.

The first real rays of hope arrived in the form of some friends of the family who came over one night to pray for me. Bob Eroshevich, who was a good friend of my brother Mark; his brother-in-law, Dr. Michael Scarpone; and the Rev. Philip Massimi, a pastor at a local church, stayed with me for a couple of hours the night before I was scheduled to begin my treatment at the Cleveland Clinic. They prayed with my mother and me.

It was a very emotional time. It was the first time that my mother and I cried together about what had happened to me. It was the first time that I remember we ever prayed in unison for something we both desperately wanted—the return of my health.

The Rev. Massimi brought with him deep spiritual guidance that was helping us to get in touch with the spiritual aspect of the ordeal. He also brought help in a more pragmatic form. He shared with us the story of his wife, who had suffered for a long time with Crohn's disease. He told us that she had recently suffered a flare-up, but she was turning the corner and beginning to heal. This was important to me because the doctors at Allegheny General had speculated that I might have Crohn's before they recommended that I seek another opinion.

Crohn's is considered the more chronic form of IBD. I had heard stories of a few people whose lives were shattered by the diagnosis of Crohn's. The disease itself is characteristic of deeper ulcerations into the intestinal wall than that of colitis, in which the ulcers are not deep into the tissue. In ulcerative colitis, one large, continuous stretch of the intestine is typically affected, while the disease appears in patchy spots all over the intestine in most cases of Crohn's. Surgery can be considered a cure for ulcerative colitis. The diseased area can be removed, and in most cases the two healthy sections of bowel can be reconnected.

There is no cure for Crohn's disease. The outlook is generally bleaker with a Crohn's diagnosis than that of ulcerative colitis, though they are similarly horrible. Crohn's tends to recur more often and in new areas of the digestive tract. The lesions in the digestive tract are deeper into the tissue than in ulcerative colitis. Other inflammatory symptoms manifest themselves in other membranes and areas of the human body such as the skin, joints, other internal organs, and even in the eyes. A diagnosis of Crohn's was something my family and I were very fearful of at this time. The Rev. Massimi's story gave me hope that if the diagnosis of Crohn's came to fruition, I could go on.

That night also helped me realize the depth of how much people can care. I had received many cards and phone calls and well wishes from many people, but this visit struck a special chord because it was forcing me to address the issue of what my faith would mean in this experience. It was also hard to push these people away as I had most of the others because they were right here in front of me. It was not like telling my mother to tell a caller that I was sleeping or leaving letters unanswered. They had God on their side, too, and I still feared God, even though my faith in God's plan was lacking at the time.

I feared the diagnosis of Crohn's as I began my treatment at the Clinic. It was Labor Day weekend of 1989. It was memorable because the Pittsburgh Steelers were getting hammered by the Cleveland Browns that day, 51-0. My dad and I watched the game in the lobby while my mother took care of the insurance paperwork to begin the admissions process.

My father and I had been Steeler fans ever since I could remember. My parents were born and raised in Pittsburgh, and being a Steeler fan seemed like a birthright. We had had season tickets for the Steeler home games since the mid-1970s. It was the era of the Steel Curtain, arguably the best football team ever assembled. My dad was becoming upset with the results of this loss against the archrival Browns, as he sometimes did. I didn't understand how sports could mean that much to him even though I was a big fan. Nothing could take my mind off the worries about what I was facing, anyway.

The doctors scheduled some tests so that they would be able to make a diagnosis. I would stay for a week, and they would watch me carefully. The first test I had to undergo was a colonoscopy. During this procedure, a long, thin tube with a scope on the end was passed through my rectum and fed through the colon. The scope's camera would take pictures of my colon while a doctor watched the pictures on a monitor in the room.

It can be a very painful procedure for someone who has inflammation of the digestive tract. Therefore, the patients are usually heavily sedated throughout the procedure, which usually lasts less than ten minutes. I was sedated, but to no effect because I was too scared to feel anything.

All I remember is the doctor saying over and over, "Oh yeah, this is Crohn's." I was crushed. Despite the amount of relaxation drugs I was on, I was shaking. I was wheeled back to my room. When my parents came in, they asked what the doctor said.

"I have Crohn's," I cried. My mother tried to hug me but I pushed her away. I just lay on the bed with a pillow on my face, sobbing. It felt like someone had hit me in the chest with a sledgehammer and knocked all the life out of me.

I ran the gamut of emotions. I was sad, angry, and scared. I felt alone. I felt as though I had let people down. I would have to fight this like I had fought opponents in the arena of athletics. This would not be just an acute episode of a disease. The rest of my life would be different.

During the next few days, I endured several more painful tests. I was oblivious to what was going on around me until one day a whole team of doctors came into my room. One of them was holding a large map. Another was holding a pointer.

They proceeded to explain to me that I had a couple of surgical options. They pointed to diagrams with a drawing of a human body's digestive tract. It seemed like a bunch of engineers testing parts in an automobile. How could they show such little concern about my life? I felt as though my body and I were being treated as an impersonal infomercial.

One of the surgical options was to have my colon completely removed and have my small bowel attached to my rectum, which was called "the small bowel hookup." The other option was to have an ileostomy pouch attached to my lower right abdomen where my small intestine could empty the digestive waste into an attached pouch.

Both procedures scared the living hell out of me. "There's no way I'll do this! Get the hell out of this room!" I yelled at the doctors. I sounded tough, but deep inside, I wondered if the doctors could actually make me have the surgery. They weren't forcing anything on me though. They were presenting the best options they knew to fight the disease. I just wanted them to stop treating me like a car.

I stood firm in my tough stand against having the surgery. My vanity about my physical being, along with my levels of stubbornness and immaturity, were at an all-time high. The ostomy would be like having a limb removed. I would rather take any kind of medication than have surgery.

When the doctors realized how set I was against the surgery, they decided to take a new approach toward my therapy. They prescribed the drug Imuran, which is a powerful immunosuppressant. It was sometimes being used as chemotherapy and was finding success with patients of IBD, but only as a last resort. Although it was prescribed for only six-to-eight week cycles, it was potentially dangerous to compromise someone's immune system by using the drug.

That didn't matter to me. I was convinced that the risk was better than the surgery. Besides, after a week in the hospital, I would be going home to give recuperation another try. My condition had not become any worse and I was able to eat, so there was no need for intravenous feeding.

I was still having frequent stools, about seven or eight per day, and the pain was now all over my abdomen, not just in the left side. I was wiped out, and my energy level was as low as it had been back in Allegheny General. The doctors did decide, however, that I could go home and try to recuperate there.

I had been home for about a week when I began having intense rectal pain when I was going to the bathroom. It wouldn't have been so bad if it were only one or two times per day, but seven or eight times was pure torture.

The diarrhea would come on suddenly, and I would scurry to the bathroom and slam the door shut. Then I would growl and scream at the top of my lungs while I was sitting on the toilet. I would sit there for at least 20 minutes each time. At first my parents would hear me screaming and yell through the door to see if I was all right. They soon became accustomed to my sound effects.

It was becoming hard for me to walk. I had so much pain and pressure in my rectum that any bodily movement, even a cough, hurt. It felt like a bowling ball was trying to push itself through the right side of my rectum. Needless to say it was time to see the doctors again to find out why I was having this pain.

My parents drove to Cleveland with me sprawled out in the back seat of the car. It hurt to sit down like a normal human being. Every bump in the road sent waves of pain through my backside. When we arrived at the hospital, there was a long wait in the lobby. I was lying with my back flat on the seat of the chair and the top of my head pressed against the chair's back. It sounds very uncomfortable, but it was the only position I could keep myself in to take the pressure off my rectum.

My mother had prearranged with the team of doctors for me to see a colorectal surgeon. The only problem was that his office was on the other side of the clinic's campus. I wasn't looking forward to the walk and after about 20 steps, I buckled over in pain. My father grabbed a wheelchair in the lobby and wheeled me across campus. I was half lying, half sitting in the chair. I screamed as every bump we hit on the sidewalk sent tremors of pain through my bottom that were felt to the tenth power. Was it only five months before that I was a 220-pound power-hitting first baseman for a Division I baseball team? The surgeon examined me and told me I would need to stay for some exploratory surgery. He didn't know what the cause of the pain was. He suspected either a severe case of hemorrhoids or an abscess. He said surgery was absolutely needed and that my arguments could have some serious implications if I waited. I was confused, scared, and angry, but I couldn't walk. What choice did I have?

When I awoke from the surgery, the doctors explained to me that they did not find an abscess, but they removed a hemorrhoid. To do this, the surgeon removed the lower right portion of my rectum. This did not seem right to me, but hey, he was a *doctor*. Who was I, a mere mortal, to argue with him? I was a fool not to because my rectum would never function the same way again.

The day following the surgery, my parents took me home from the hospital. After a day at home, the thunder-and-lightning-like pain returned to my rectum. It wasn't from the surgical scarring. Something else was wrong. Another bumpy, painful two-hour ride to Cleveland was scheduled for the next day.

When I saw the surgeon, I explained that the painful pressure had returned. The surgeon was very quiet. He would not make eye contact with me.

"I think you have an abscess," he said softly.

"I thought you said that you didn't see an abscess?" I asked him.

"I must have missed it," he replied.

He went on to explain that abscesses are very dangerous if they are not drained immediately. The potential for side effects is great, and in extreme cases, death can occur if one works its way into the bloodstream and travels to the brain. He urged me to permit him to treat it with an emergency surgery.

Again, it seemed as though I had no choice. Not only was I again totally incapacitated, but I was also playing with fire if I left the abscess untreated. The same doctor performed the surgery.

When I awoke from the surgery, I had two tubes inserted in the right inside wall of my rectum to induce drainage of the abscess. It was the surgical method of choice for that particular surgeon. I would later find out that it was a bad choice.

The tubes were uncomfortable, but they eased the pain and the pressure gradually. The doctors warned me not to sit in water that was too hot because they thought I might irritate the tissue. I suggested that the heat might draw out the fluid faster, but the doctors said "No." I still had to sit in a sitz bath after each of the eight trips I was making to the bathroom each day. After another week-long stay in the hospital, I went home.

Physically, I was at my lowest point. I weighed 150 pounds and was bedridden. I could crawl to the bathroom, but that was the only time I could move — when I was forced to. I was still having trouble controlling my bowels because the muscle tissue at the end of my digestive tract was badly diseased, surgically under repair, and in one spot, no longer there. I was going through anywhere from five to ten Depends a day.

In college, my friends and I used to joke about older people using Depends. Suddenly at the age of 22, I was in worse shape than many older people. For some reason, this time my huge ego did not get in the way of the treatment of this humiliating disease. There had been many other occasions in these several months that I normally would have considered embarrassing.

I soiled myself many times, I was subject to much poking and prodding during numerous examinations, my private parts were exposed during nearly all of the examinations, and people didn't recognize me the few times I went out in public. In front of people I was able to put on a brave face.

Privately I wasn't so tough, though. I argued with my parents about my treatment, and I became increasingly surly and bitter. I babied myself too much. I know that at that point, I hadn't come to the realization that Crohn's disease never goes away. Even though the situation was starting to become desperate, deep down inside I had a belief that something good had to come from all of this.

In the two weeks following the surgery, my condition still had not improved. I was struggling to get out of bed, still having a great deal of pain and diarrhea, and my weight was still only 150. The Imuran wasn't working, and my family and I were becoming more and more frustrated and worried about my prognosis. I really needed something to change.

The concerned calls kept coming to our house. Coach Carbone had been urging me to continue my treatment at the Ohio State Medical School's Hospital. It just so happened that the head of the gastroenterology department there was Fred Thomas. Fred's son, Tim, had been a teammate of mine during my last year at Ohio U. Coach Carbone talked to Dr.

Thomas about me, and Dr. Thomas said he was pretty confident that he could help me get turned around. It was a ray of hope shining through my darkest hour.

My mother called Dr. Thomas, probably in a panic, the way most loving mothers would. She had been outstanding and very devoted at finding the answers for me and talking to doctors. She felt she had some answers after she talked to Dr. Thomas. He told my mother that there were some adjustments that needed to be made in my treatment and that he would like to see me soon for an examination.

There was no decision to make. All the trips to hospitals were far from my parents' home in Steubenville. Allegheny General was one hour, Cleveland Clinic was two, and Ohio State was nearly three. Car trips were very uncomfortable for me, and we often had to stop to go to the bathroom. Sometimes I didn't make it to a bathroom in time. It was plain to see, however, if I was going to get any semblance of a life back, the longer drive to OSU would be worth it. I needed more help than I was getting in Cleveland.

Dr. Thomas more than provided the help. He was very easygoing, friendly, and genuinely concerned about me. He was also very knowledgeable. He put me back on prednisone, assuring me that I could take a higher dose for a period of time and later taper off the drug at a slower rate than the first time. He prescribed iron and folic acid supplements, which were necessary to stabilize my blood and nutrient levels. He also prescribed Imodium to slow down my bowels. That made sense. The other doctors had said elixirs wouldn't help.

Dr. Thomas assured my family and me that we could call him any time if I had any problems. He made me feel like I was special. I definitely did not feel as though he thought I was a car with a bad colon.

Another good thing Dr. Thomas said was that he did not believe that I needed to be hospitalized. He also said we could wait to do tests because from the symptoms, it was obvious to him that I had Crohn's. It was such a relief. Finally, there was some light at the end of the tunnel.

Back home again, I finally started to feel better after a few weeks. The tubes fell out, and my rectum started to heal. I was getting around the house better after several weeks of being bedridden. Dr. Thomas also suggested that I start exercising again in December.

# Chapter Seven

# A Real Thanksgiving

# CHAPTER SEVEN — A REAL THANKSGIVING

As Thanksgiving of 1989 approached, it was very evident that I had a lot to be thankful for. I had a great family and many friends who were rooting for me during my recovery, but the attention made me uncomfortable. I didn't want anyone focusing on what I perceived to be a weakness in my character. When friends would visit or ask about my prognosis, I acted as though there were no problems. I did not let on to anyone how bad the situation really was. Part of me had always been fearful of illness and people with physical maladies, and now I had a whole new perspective on being physically challenged. But these people were with me all the way.

I wondered if I would be able to be an active, normal person again. Dr. Thomas assured me that I would be able to do anything I wanted to do, as long as I felt well and kept taking the medication. I had hoped to start lifting weights again with the intention of building myself back up to the muscular build I had before the symptoms began. I had golfed some when I was younger, and I wanted to do that, too. I also was fascinated with martial arts, and I wanted to study them in some form.

Finishing my undergraduate degree was my top priority. I wanted to make a deeper commitment to academics than I had before. I knew I needed a college education to have a decent occupational future.

A couple of people asked me about getting into coaching. I had always been opposed to the idea. In the last couple of years, I had started to think of baseball as a job. Most 22-year-old-people should think of baseball as a fun game. I had put so much pressure on myself to do well and get drafted again that I made myself miserable. As my last year was ending, I had said I wanted nothing to do with baseball. After seeing Dr. Thomas and receiving some hope, however, I was really missing the game.

Coach Carbone told me he wanted me to come and work with the first basemen when I went back to school in January. I started to think that might be fun. Also, the DeLucas had purchased a bar in Athens. Danny and Ronnie would be running the bar, and they told me I could work for them to make money to help pay my bills.

In the meantime, Mark Stacy let me do some work at his convenience store, labeling prices on products. Many people were reaching out to me, trying to help me get back on my feet. I tried to pass off the attention, to play it cool, as if there were nothing wrong with me. Again, as always, I just wanted so much to be normal. Even though it appeared on the outside that I was getting better, the pain and the other symptoms still occurred to remind me that I had a long way to go.

By Thanksgiving, I was starting to gain weight again. Many of my friends were home from college. That meant everyone would be getting together for parties. The big question was whether or not I would be able to drink again.

Drinking had been a large part of my social life before I became sick. The only thing that could have stopped me from drinking then was to have a severe digestive disorder. An ulcer would not have been enough. There were times when I drank through having colds, sinus infections, the flu, and other afflictions that most human beings are beset with throughout the normal course of their lives. No neurological malady would have stopped me. No muscular-skeletal disease would have stopped me. Not liver disease or even cancer. It had to be a condition that made me nauseated to ingest anything by mouth, and Crohn's disease is the best thing to make a human being that sick.

I was on the road to recovery. Deep down, I believed that I would be 100 percent healthy again someday. At the end of November, I decided that if I could begin exercising again, I could try to resume the rest of my normal behavior.

I wasn't going to be foolish about it. Well, really I was because anything more than a couple drinks for anyone is foolish. It was even more stupid for someone who had a condition that could be exacerbated by drinking and might help necessitate the surgical removal of a major organ. It seemed that every person I knew that was my age drank. I didn't see any other social options.

Dr. Thomas said before that I could have a couple beers, and he stressed only if I felt okay. Before I became ill, to me, one or two used to mean nine or ten. A few would mean twelve or so. That was then and this was reality. I had a few beers two or three times and it didn't feel very good.

For the rest of the holiday season, I felt so-so. My weight was up a little, and that was a good sign, but I was still far below what my normal weight should have been. My face was bloated and full of acne from the steroids. I was very conscious of my appearance, and I knew I didn't look good despite the fact that people told me that I did just to make me feel better. Although I was very much in denial, it was clear to others that it would take a miracle for me to return to 100 percent.

After Christmas, I had a decision to make. I would either go back to school to finish the last year of my degree program or put it off until spring and stay home to try to make myself feel better. After deliberating with my parents, I chose to stay home. I would return to school in late March.

From January through March, my condition stayed pretty much the same. It was hard for me to go out in public because of the fear that I wouldn't make it to the bathroom in time. Combined with the severe weight loss and other changes my body had been through, socializing was a tough ordeal for me.

When the end of March 1990 finally came, I returned to Ohio U. with mixed emotions. I was tired of being cooped up in my bedroom at my parents' house. I felt like I needed more stimulation than watching the Pittsburgh Penguins' hockey games on television. I was scared that the embarrassing symptoms from which I suffered would become known to my roommates and friends. I wondered if I would be fatigued just walking to class. I hoped I would be able to eat properly. I was concerned about the way I looked and about how my friends would react to my drinking only two beers instead of what I used to do.

Dr. Thomas continuously reassured me that everything would be all right. He made me feel confident that I could function as a normal human being. That meant a lot to me, especially considering the premium I had always placed on being "normal." I was also confident that, in Dr. Thomas, I had a special friend who would do anything in his power to help me get better. If anything went wrong, Columbus was only a little more than an hour from Athens.

Classes were going well. I took just enough hours to retain full-time status. The lighter load and having no baseball practice to go to every day made me want to spend time studying. My grades would reflect this at the end of the quarter.

Inside my mind, though, things weren't always so good. My friends and roommates couldn't understand why I slept so much or why I went to the bathroom so much. They especially couldn't understand why I was so moody. They were pretty good about the drinking, but I still felt like I had to drink as much as I used to to fit in.

Coach Carbone called and explained the things he thought I could help with if I would come to practice to help out coaching a little. He was trying to give me something in my life to give me direction and a sense of purpose. My chance to help the team would be put on hold for the time being, however.

I was ready to go to practice when I started to feel very ill again. All of the symptoms returned, albeit to a lesser degree than the first time. I had foolishly tried to be normal again and fit in with college students by partying, eating junk food, and neglecting sleep at the wrong times. Normal behavior was not going to help me overcome an abnormal condition.

Dr. Thomas told me to get to Columbus quickly because I was losing weight at a rapid pace. I was very embarrassed that this was happening to me again. I was rude with people who asked about my health. I was even starting to become rude to the health care professionals who were trying to help me. It was hard for me to remain patient with the same questions about my weight, bathroom trips, and energy level.

It is tough to deliver bad news to people all the time, especially when the news is about your own health. I became even more adept at deflecting attention from myself. Before, I was ashamed because I didn't want to tell people I was chasing a dream that could leave me flat on my face if I failed. Since the illness, I was ashamed because of my self-perceived "weakness."

I would tell people I was doing okay and immediately ask about them, their families, their schoolwork or job, and the rest of a list of rhetorical, meaningless questions that I had subconsciously scripted to divert attention from my health. This didn't matter to the nurses and aides who were sent in before the doctors to find information. They were being paid to find out about me.

My lack of cooperation with the health care people wasn't helping my condition. I wanted to talk only to Dr. Thomas. He reviewed the new symptoms that I was having, and he speculated that I might have some type of bacterial infection. Some of the things that were happening were atypical of a Crohn's flare-up. Fortunately, the tests confirmed this, and

Dr. Thomas prescribed a short course of antibiotics that would help me feel better.

"Better" to me meant to be totally free of symptoms. As I finished that quarter of school, I was still in a state of denial. It was still less than a year after being diagnosed, and in my heart I believed that nothing less than a return to 100 percent full health was imminent. Dr. Thomas knew how I felt and explained to me more than a couple times that the disease could be controlled but not cured. I foolishly believed that I was different and that I was so tough that I could make the disease go away.

Despite the fact that this latest episode was very hard on me, I still failed to realize that I was not a normal human being. Most normal people do not lose more than 20 pounds from a simple infection. My state of health was so fragile that any type of adverse condition I might acquire could potentially be devastating to me. I went from thinking I was so tough to being fragile in less than a year, but my ego would never permit me to admit that. I was in deep denial.

I went back to Steubenville for the summer. Matt Morrison was starting his coaching career with our legion team. A couple people involved with the legion, including Mark Stacy, asked if I would be interested in helping out.

I still had mixed feelings about coaching. I thought that I knew enough baseball to have something to offer, but coaching didn't seem to thrill me. I believed what some people said about the "Can't do? Teach!/Can't play? Coach!" theory. I didn't like the idea of having to discipline kids. I feared what people might think of me.

It was again about my self-perception. I thought any situation in which I might look bad would have to be avoided. I was boxing myself into a corner. Another dynamic of my behavior was that I attempted to keep my privacy by not participating in social activities.

Friends would call and say, "We're going to a game," or "Let's go to a concert," and I would decline. I always had a lame excuse prepared. They couldn't understand why I wouldn't go anywhere.

I couldn't explain to them that I was still mostly sick, although sometimes I felt better. I was too embarrassed by the symptoms. I didn't want to be perceived as "weak." I was angry and frustrated. I felt no one understood. I never had a reputation for being an overly "nice" guy, and I was doing nothing to dispute that perception.

# Chapter Eight

# Fighting Two Wars

## CHAPTER EIGHT — FIGHTING TWO WARS

I still had about 30 hours worth of credits to graduate. The DeLucas were kind enough to permit me to work at their business and not be too demanding with me. They were trying to help me get back on my feet like everyone else was. There were still some friends of mine taking classes, but I didn't want to share an apartment with anyone. The symptoms were too embarrassing, and the thought of having a bathroom occupied by a roommate for a long time while I might need to use it embarrassed me. Plus, I needed to sleep a lot. It was hard for me to explain this to anyone.

Going to the bathroom had become the primary focus of my life. Even when the disease was in its more quiescent stages, I still went to the bathroom four times per day. Sometimes the trips would be urgent. I never would grow accustomed to this. I was very uncomfortable using the bathroom in any public place, so I was limited on the amount of traveling I tried to do.

I lived in fear of being at work or in class or anywhere and having to go to the bathroom and not making it in time. If I didn't make it in time, I would go home and clean up without a problem and no one knew because there would be no one home. It made for a lonely existence.

I refused to go to support groups. I thought I was too tough for a psychologist. I thought I would take the pills, do what the doctors said, and everything would be fine. I knew for sure that I didn't want an ostomy in any way, shape, or form. I thought I was doing what all good patients did and that was just take the pills so I could get back to "normal."

I continued to progress toward my degree with the hope of being able to someday find a "normal" job. School went pretty well in the fall of '90. I had a couple B's, an A, and a C. Working at the bar gave me a chance to socialize a little bit. The urge to drink was still there, and Danny DeLuca, some friends at the bar, and I would have a few beers after work. Another good friend of ours, Ed Gaughan, had just finished his undergraduate degree at Kent State and moved to Athens with aspirations of earning a graduate degree, but I still was feeling more out of place.

When I went home for Christmas break that year, I was starting to sense that people were uncomfortable around me. They didn't know what to say without getting me upset. I was on the edge all the time, partially as a side effect of the prednisone, partially from my poor self-perception, and partially from just plain feeling awful.

I talked to a  priest at confession about this. He told me that my anger was not indicative of my being a bad person but rather a reaction people have sometimes to becoming ill. I found little consolation in this explanation. I feared that people would see me as a bitter, sick person, and that no one would want to be around me. Paradoxically, I was still pushing people away. I could not pour my heart out to anyone without feeling weak emotionally.

The person I was before I became ill was gone. I felt that I had no identity. I had been concerned about partying, baseball, and occasionally women. There was none of that now. My license to be a jerk had expired since the cheering had stopped, and I was too sick to be as carefree about my partying as I had been before. I had no identity.

Some of my friends were not missing a beat though, and I envied them. They still were going at it full speed ahead. It was like I was forced to sit out of a game and watch it from the press box. I had a great view but I didn't like what I saw.

About this time, I started to become more depressed. I began reflecting on my short time on earth. I asked myself some tough questions. What was my purpose? Why did I make the awful choices I made? Why did I have such a surly, distrustful disposition? I started to regret many of the things I had done in my life to that point, not giving baseball a better effort, like not having more confidence in all things I tried, and especially partying too much.

Right after Christmas, I went off prednisone for the first time in more than a year. Almost immediately, the pain, cramping, diarrhea, and fatigue increased, but not as severely as before. The next quarter of classes at Ohio U. was to start in early January of 1991, and the return of the symptoms and the depressing feelings that had begun to surface compounded my anxiety about returning to do school work.

After a week of classes, the symptoms were significantly worse. I knew I needed to see Dr. Thomas, but I feared being admitted to the hospital. It was ironic because at the time, the United States was fighting the Gulf War and I was fighting two wars: one with my colon and one with my mind.

My mother and father were urging me to see Dr. Thomas, but I couldn't pull the trigger. I refused to believe that the disease was flaring up on me. Deep down inside, I thought that these Crohn's flare-ups that I read about in health journals happened to people who were not tough enough to defeat them. I'll show them, I thought. I'll never have to stay in the hospital again.

During the second week of classes, however, the symptoms became overpowering. I was in bed for 16 hours a day and barely eating. I still ignored my parents' pleas. Then one day, I began vomiting uncontrollably.

This scared me because the disease had been confined to my lower digestive tract. Vomiting was a rarity for me, and it can be symptomatic of upper intestinal involvement in Crohn's. When the disease is present in both the lower and upper parts of the intestinal tract, the disease is twice as miserable with more serious implications. It was one of the main reasons that surgery didn't seem like an option to me. I could wind up with the ostomy and still be sick. Not even the bloody stools were enough for me to call Dr. Thomas. The occurrence of the vomiting was the only thing that prompted me to finally make the call. Sometimes God sends bad situations for good reasons.

I finally talked to Dr. Thomas, and he told me to get to OSU immediately. I didn't want to ask anyone to help me. I was too stubborn and embarrassed. I decided to drive myself to Columbus.

The disease had manifested in my rectum again. It was very painful for me to sit, so I set off to make the 90-minute drive from Athens to Columbus with the driver's seat fully reclined to take pressure off my rear end. What a sight I must have been to other motorists on Route 33 that day, looking like I was a small child driving the car from the backseat. I drove 45 miles per hour the whole way up, and often times I was further under the speed limit. The only time I came close to having an accident, thank God, was not in the car but in my pants when I pulled into a gas station in the city of Lancaster to barely make it to the bathroom in time.

After a few tests, Dr. Thomas prescribed the usual protocol of intravenous steroids, liquids, and other medications and reassured me that I would be back to action soon. It was important that I had come when I did because I had another abscess that had to be drained. Without the vomiting, I would have still been waiting to call Dr. Thomas, and the abscess could have done serious damage.

The doctors had no explanation for the episode of vomiting, which ended almost immediately after I made the phone call to Dr. Thomas. But getting there when I did led the doctors to be able to identify and surgically drain the abscess before it caused serious damage. Fortunately, I had avoided another potential disaster.

After a week in the hospital I was released in time to go home for Super Bowl XXV, featuring the New York Giants against the Buffalo Bills. I remember feeling sorry for Scott Norwood, the Bills' kicker, who missed the field goal late in the game that would have made the Bills champions. In the past, I would have ridiculed him as many fans did. The things I was going through gave me a different perspective on sports.

I don't think that I really appreciated the things that make competitive sports as great as they are before I became ill. As I aged, I enjoyed sports only because I was good at them. There were many other things that I was beginning again to enjoy about sports. The camaraderie, the hard work and sacrifice, the spotlight, achieving a goal, thrilling upset victories, heartbreaking disappointments, and sheer artistry had also been lost in my search for instant physical, social, and emotional gratification through partying. Sports had become only a form of entertainment to watch and occupational for me to participate in as my attitude and health declined before the onset of the disease.

At least from the time I had to think while lying on my back, an appreciation for sports was beginning to resurface. I was also starting to realize that other people were suffering, and I was finally becoming sensitive to their misfortunes. The first time I was in the hospital in Allegheny General, I cried only twice in 35 days despite all the physical pain, emotional duress, sadness, and anxiety from my family and myself.

One of the times I cried was when Dave Dravecky, the San Francisco Giants pitcher who overcame a cancerous tumor in his pitching arm, broke that arm in the second start of his comeback. Things like that had never fazed me before. At least through my suffering, I was able to empathize with others who were going through tough times. Dravecky's story meant a lot to me, and it showed me what courage and character were all about. It made me think that maybe there were worse things than being in the hospital for 35 straight days.

As I watched the Dravecky story from my hospital bed, I was more violently ill than I had ever been before in my life. Yet seeing another human being suffer made me more sad than I had been about my own situation, and I had never even met this man.

The illness was changing things for the better in that respect. I was starting to feel sensitive, human emotions for the first time since I was a child. It took a long time, but now I feel things much more deeply than before. I choke up every time I watch *Field of Dreams* during the scene Kevin Costner asks the actor playing his father if they can play catch at the end of the movie. I get chills up my spine when I hear songs like "The Rain Song" by Led Zepplin, Bob Seger's "Travellin' Man/ Beautiful Loser," and Chicago's "(I've Been) Searchin' So Long," to name a few. These things never happened to me before the illness. Many of these emotions are evoked by sporting events.

Since I was going through a second bout with the illness, it was becoming evident that my emotional outlook was not the only thing that had to change. I would have to make some modifications in my diet, my exercise regimen, my belief in the purpose and necessity of the prescribed medication, and the belief that I would one day again be 100 percent healthy.

I acquiesced to my mother's strong suggestions that I drop out of school for the quarter and move back to Steubenville to live with my parents. I still had the possibility of graduating in the spring, and I had set my sights on going to graduate school. I knew I should not have plans to do anything that necessitated finishing my degree in a hurry. I stayed at home and began to heal again

Part of the healing process involved exercising. Before I became ill, I always took my energy level for granted. Now, exercising was physically draining for me even while the disease was in remission. I knew that the exercising needed to be done. It relieved stress for a while and helped my self-esteem. I needed that the most because I didn't feel like myself when I weighed only 150 or 160 pounds. This was despite the fact that I received the usual rhetorical compliments about how good I looked.

So again, I went at it with the weights. Slowly, my body weight came back and I began feeling better. I gained weight with the help of the prednisone, which made my appetite enormous. It was also the only anti-inflammatory agent that seemed to settle the disease down from its active stages.

When the disease finally reached a stable stage of remission, I returned to Ohio U. to finish my undergradraduate degree. Finally after a long struggle, I received my B.S. in journalism at the end of spring in

1991. It was the first good thing that had happened to me in a while. Although I felt a sense of achievement, it wasn't anything to rest on because I didn't see myself using the degree in the field. I was feeling that athletics were somehow calling me back.

I applied to graduate school several times before I was accepted into Ohio U.'s education administration program. The DeLucas gave me the part-time bartending job once again to help with my bills. I went to the baseball office at the beginning of September to ask Coach Carbone if I could help the team in any way.

I didn't really know what I wanted to do. Maybe keep score. Maybe be an equipment manager. Coach Carbone kept suggesting coaching. They had a graduate assistant, Jack Hatem, but they needed to add one coach to make the staff complete. I decided to take Coach Carbone's advice and spend the year coaching.

I greatly appreciated the chance. I knew that Coach Carbone and Coach Toadvine were trying to help me and give me some direction. I don't know if I would fully understand the help they gave me until much later.

The six weeks of practice in the fall went well. I started to learn a lot about coaching at the college level. It was much more involved than I thought it would be, especially on the administrative side. There were many NCAA rules to be followed, and meticulous planning was needed to organize every practice minute for three hours every day for each of the 35 players on the team. I always thought that we just showed up at practice, took some ground balls, hit a little, ran a little, and went home. There are also recruiting, scheduling, budget management, fundraising, academic counseling, eligibility paperwork, and being a parent/cheerleader/disciplinarian/psychologist. The experience was an eye-opener for me. It changed the way I looked at coaching.

I never fully understood the rewards that coaching could bring. My previous thought pattern allowed me to see only the negative things. I learned many things that year. I learned much about people and I learned more about myself. I learned I had something to offer to people. Some of the players told me that they learned a lot from me and that they thought I was a good communicator.

I had a lot to learn about the game. You never stop learning about baseball until you die. It was finally becoming evident that I possessed some skills that might identify a professional purpose in my life. I started to think very seriously about entering into the coaching field to earn a living.

Graduate school went well. My training in the journalism program helped develop my written and oral communication skills that were necessary to do the work in the program I was taking. The training gave me an edge over some of the other students because I had learned the nuances of presenting not only thoughts and ideas but also myself, in a positive, professional manner. I started to believe in myself a little bit more, but I had a long way to go.

We finished the 1992 season at Ohio U. as runner-up in the Mid-American Conference. I saw firsthand the things that are needed to be a champion. We were just a little short on talent. Kent State had several dominating players that made the difference for them and allowed them to beat us for the championship.

One of the players Kent State had was their third baseman, Mike Gulan. He was named MAC player of the year in 1992 because of the two great years he had as a sophomore and a junior. A part of me was rooting for him as we battled Kent State for the championship.

Mike had grown up in Steubenville. He was four years younger than me. He and my brother Tim were good friends and played sports together. Mike and Jamie Taylor, who was from our area and starred at Ohio State, had awesome college baseball careers. They went far into the tryouts for the United States Olympic baseball team before they were cut on the final day. I think the things that my teammates and I were able to do helped show them earlier that maybe guys from Steubenville could be pretty good ballplayers, after all.

One of the memories I will always have from the 1992 season was one game we played at Kent. Mike had a bad game. He left several runners on base in key situations. The expression on his face, however, was the same one he wore during a game in which he had three hits against us and led his team to a win.

I never had that confidence as a player. Every small failure was devastating to me. Tim McCarver, the catcher-turned-baseball-announcer once said that every at-bat for Paul O'Neil, the volatile New York Yankees outfielder, was "Armageddon." It was the same to me. I would battle with my whole heart and soul in competitive situations, but I never had 100 percent confidence that I would succeed. That was the biggest difference between guys like Mike and me. I lacked the confidence that they had, not only in baseball but in all facets of life.

Having to live with Crohn's disease should have given me confidence. It was not easy to discipline myself to moderate my diet, to take the medication religiously, to get enough rest, to live with the embarrassing symptoms, to juggle the rigors of taking classes, work another job part-time, and coaching. Despite the fact that I was doing all of these successfully, I was starting to feel only a little better about myself.

Although I was physically feeling better, I felt as though I was always looking over my shoulder to see if another flare-up was gaining on me. Sometimes it was just the moodiness that the disease and the steroids contributed to. Other times it was that natural human reaction to fear of the unknown, especially wondering what my future would be like after taking the medications that could have unknown side effects.

One problem with medication's side effects occurred during the fall of that year. Dr. Thomas had decided to try a cycle of an immunosuppressant drug that was similar to 6-mp, which I had taken with no success at the Cleveland Clinic. Dr. Thomas was concerned about a colon scope I'd had done a few months earlier.

The scope had shown that there was a lot of damage that the disease was still doing to my colon. The pictures taken by the scope were sickening. There was a gross amount of inflammation. There were also many pseudopolyps, which are basically nonmalignant polyps that look like bulbs protruding from a human being's internal organs. There was also some mucosal bridging, which occurs when some tissue is torn from a side of the colon but is still connected or "bridged" at the top and bottom. Also, most people have a colon that is the shade of their tongue and inside of their mouth. My colon was a ghostly gray-white. It was a horrific sight, and Dr. Thomas and I agreed that we needed to take a more aggressive approach with the medication.

This time, I had a strange reaction to the immunosuppressive. I began to feel pain in the top of my skull and in my shinbones. It began a few days after the dose started with the new medication, so I knew that it was a side effect that was unforeseen by the doctors.

We were just finishing our fall baseball practice at the time so I had a little down time. I had just taken midterm exams in my first semester of grad school. When I told Dr. Thomas what was happening, he suggested that I wait a few days to see if the symptoms were from a virus because the pain I was having was not a normal (there's that word again) side effect from the medication.

After two more days, the pain was sharper and more consistent. The pain in my shins made it difficult to walk. I have never had my head in a vise grip before, but I can't imagine that pain would be much greater than what I was experiencing. I called Dr. Thomas again, and he urged me to check in to OSU Medical Hospital for some tests.

When I was admitted, I underwent the usual tests and 50 questions. The doctors insisted that they could find only one other documented case of such symptoms in over ten years of treatment using the drug for inflammatory bowel disease. They prescribed taking a break from the medication for a while to see what happened. I was sure ceasing the cycle would be the answer. The pain was so great and constant that I was sure it was not a virus or even the normal Crohn's flare-up symptoms.

After a couple days of observation, the pain went away. The doctors were surprised because the reaction was so rare. But now that I could not take the drug, what would happen to all the inflammation and active disease in my colon? We went back on the normal medication: Sulfasalazine, Flagyl, and 15 milligrams of prednisone. We waited and hoped for improvement.

It seemed like every time there was a reason for hope, something went wrong. I suffered many of these disappointments. They chopped away at my confidence just like every hitless at-bat in baseball. Every bad report from Dr. Thomas was "Armageddon." I was wondering if the rest of my life would be filled with regular, tension-filled doctor visits, sickness, depression, and, of course, the threat of having a colectomy done.

# Chapter Nine

# That Word

# CHAPTER NINE — THAT WORD

I finished my masters' degree in the summer of 1992. I did much better in graduate school than I had done in my undergrad. I had mostly A's and four or five B's. I had no idea about finding a job though. In what? I thought about coaching, maybe trying to get into entry level college administration, maybe teaching, maybe writing, maybe starting doctoral work at another college.

I moved back to my parents' home in Steubenville. My father had some friends at the University of Pittsburgh, so I explored some opportunities there. I was not able to find the right fit, however, so I continued to work odd jobs.

During Christmas vacations from college, I had worked at the post office to earn spending money. In the late fall of 1992, it looked like a chance for me to do the same while sending out resumes. I applied and was hired for an indefinite period of part-time employment.

I thought that it might last for a few weeks or maybe around Christmas time until I could find a full-time job. Someone would hire me, right? I had a master's degree. I had sent resumes everywhere. My friends and schoolmates were getting jobs. My turn would surely be next.

Christmas came and went. I received no calls for interviews. I was starting to lose self-esteem because I did not have a job. I was starting to feel sorry for myself, and I was becoming skeptical about my future. Every little setback, every letter I received from a school or business saying "thanks, but no thanks," was becoming a bigger defeat. Some people suggested that I should consider making the post office a career.

Those suggestions did not excite me at all. I had attended school for too long not to somehow put my degrees to use. The "P.O." was not a healthy environment for someone who was depressed. The job is routine and unexciting. There is not much conversation or interaction. Many employees stand in one place for long periods of time. Rarely are the employees praised. It is just not the nature of the job; there is also pressure to cancel the stamps and get the mail sorted and back out in a timely fashion. The light of the sun is rarely seen except occasionally by the workers who pull the mail off the delivery trucks. It was a bad environment for me to be in.

In January, I had become weary of working at the post office. I didn't put much effort into the work and it was noticeable. One day the supervisor called me into her office.

"Mike, what is your problem?" she asked.

I tried to look at her as though I didn't know what she was talking about.

"What do you mean?" I asked.

"Well, I have received some reports about poor performance on your part. If you want to stay on and have a chance at full-time employment, you are going to have to work much harder," she said.

There was no question in my mind that she was right. I hadn't been putting in a very good effort. I wasn't challenged by the job and it bored me. I felt no sense of achievement, and my self-esteem continued to sink. I wanted to be at the post office about as much as I wanted to have a digital rectal exam done.

The fact that someone told me that I was not good at something still bothered me though. Everything bothers you when your self-esteem is low, even the things that you don't usually care about as much.

My plans for finishing the month of January at the post office and then beginning to look for a job were suddenly cut short. I received a phone call from Dr. Stevenson (a surgeon whom Dr. Thomas advised me to see the previous November) as a precautionary measure in case of an emergency. He suggested that I go back to Dr. Thomas to have more tests done.

We made arrangements to have a barium x-ray done in Columbus. I would have to take a day off from work, which was no big deal. The test was an all-day affair that required the patient to drink almost a half-gallon of chalky, milky, radioactive dye that passes through the intestines so that x-rays will show up in the digestive tract. It tasted like raw eggs mixed with milk-of-magnesia, despite the ploy from the nurses to compare the taste to a strawberry milkshake.

After I was finished with the drink, the x-rays were done in the late morning. I got dressed and waited outside Dr. Thomas' office while he saw other patients and waited for the x-rays to come back from the lab.

I didn't think much of the test. It was just like many of the others I had been through. It was uncomfortable, painful, humiliating, and tiresome. I never complained about them too much, though. That was probably because I had a tiny amount of faith somewhere deep in my heart that I would be okay someday and that God had a plan for my life. This faith was small but I know it was always there. As Dr. Thomas came out of his office, this faith was about to take a big jolt.

Usually when Dr. Thomas would first see my parents and me for an appointment, he would be jovial and make small talk for at least a few minutes before we got down to business. He always had a smile and a warm handshake for us. This time, however, he looked much different. His face wore a deadpan look. He strode quickly by us and was carrying the x-rays.

"Hi, Dr. Thomas," I said with a quizzical, hopeful expression.

"Follow me," was all he said in return.

I was puzzled by his stoic demeanor. My parents and I walked behind him down the hallway in silence. He stopped at the end of the corridor and placed the three x-rays in frames and turned on the lights.

"Take a look at these," he said. "These are not good at all."

He took a pen and circled two areas on the pictures of my colon. One was a large indentation in my descending colon and the other a smaller indentation near my sigmoid colon. In both spots my colon looked as if there were chunks on the outer lining missing.

"What are these?" I asked.

"Whatever they are, this is bad," Dr. Thomas replied. "It may be strictures—which are narrowings of the intestines that are characteristic of Crohn's—or tumors."

"Tumors?" I asked. "How can we be sure? I thought the last biopsies came out all right."

"We can't be sure," Dr. Thomas said. "Sometimes tumors grow deep in the tissue, and can't be reached by biopsies until they reach the surface and it is too late. They may start metastasizing before then, though, and I strongly believe we must act soon."

"Does this happen often with Crohn's?" I asked, fearfully hoping that somehow the odds would be on my side.

"It usually doesn't happen so quickly in a 25-year-old man but there are 25-year-olds who get colon cancer," Dr. Thomas said. "We can't be sure what we are dealing with. If you were a 45-year-old man, there is no question that this would be colon cancer."

I was numb. I didn't know what to say and neither did my parents. Dr. Thomas started to talk about other tests that could be done to try to confirm what these two spots were, but his voice blurred into a monotone while my mind drifted. I heard only one word inside my head over and over.

"Cancer…cancer…cancer…."

It was all I thought about until I heard the word I most dreaded.

"Colectomy."

Somewhere toward the end of his explanation, Dr. Thomas said the word. I knew that if *he* said it, it meant I was in big trouble. He knew how opposed I was to the surgery.

"Colectomy?" I snapped out of the haze I was in.

"Mike, it is time. We have done all we can do," Dr. Thomas said.

"I would rather die," I snapped.

I looked out the window. We were high above the ground, and I wished I had the guts to jump out headfirst into the parking lot.

"You don't mean that, Mike," Dr. Thomas said.

For a minute, I realized how idiotic I sounded. Dr. Thomas fully understood how precious life was. He was trying to give me my life back, and I was so egotistical that I didn't appreciate it.

"What about the possibility of a resection being done?" I asked. I might be able to live with that. A resection does not necessitate an ostomy appliance.

"Not in your case, Mike," Dr. Thomas replied. "Your colon is so damaged by the disease that it would be like trying to sew two wet pieces of tissue paper together. Resection is not an option for you."

"No way. No way," I snapped. "I'll never, ever, want to live like that."

That quote told a lot about my outlook and my perception of what life was all about. Having an ostomy is nothing more than a better way to go to the bathroom for people who have suffered damage to their digestive or urinary tract. Period. For me, at that time, it was a disgrace to my ego, which was always trying to convince me that I had to be perfect.

My body was the one thing that I felt I had over many of my friends. Most of them had become less active because they had jobs. When I compared myself to them, my blind, egotistical mindset told me that my body (when I was in good shape) was perfect, even though I was far from it.

I would later come to believe that God creates all human beings with many perfect imperfections. No one is totally healthy. Whether it is acne, arthritis, sinusitis, diabetes, congestion, cancer, cavities, chemical dependency, pattern baldness, insomnia, skin lesions, pulled muscles, nearsightedness, or whatever, no one is perfectly healthy. I think we are all created in our perfect God's likeness; therefore, we are all perfectly imperfect.

I couldn't fathom that at the time. I seriously wanted to be dead if surgery was my only option. All I wanted at the time was an out—an excuse to delay the inevitable. My parents and I sat in silence until I finally said, "I want a second opinion."

To my surprise, Dr. Thomas said he encouraged that. He was extremely confident that this was the right thing for me, and that other gastroenterologists would tell me the same thing.

"Either way, I'll still treat you, Mike," Dr. Thomas said. "Go get a second opinion and call me back. I'll see you again in a few weeks if you want."

"Let's go home," I said to my parents.

I realized after all the ups and downs that I had experienced in the three-plus years that I had been suffering that doctors could be wrong. In this instance, however, I should have known that this was just wishful thinking.

As we drove the three hours to home in silence, I could only hope that there was another option. My mother offered to make an appointment with her doctor, Toby Graham, a specialist at Presbyterian University Hospital in Pittsburgh.

It was typical of my parents. They always tried to do anything they could to make me comfortable while I played the spoiled child role. They put up with my silence, temper tantrums, and demands to make me comfortable.

Chronic health problems cannot help but change a person's personality. I reverted to the shy, reticent kid that I was when I was younger. The moodiness led to silence. I didn't feel the need to share my misery.

Dr. Thomas assured me that even if I had cancer, it would be slow-growing. I could go through another battery of tests to confirm or refute his fears. The tests would be scheduled several weeks apart, and they would be painful, so there was recuperation time needed in between. My mother sacrificed an upcoming appointment with Dr. Graham so I could go in her spot.

When I first met Toby Graham, she was one of the most impressive people I had ever met in my life. She walked quickly and spoke just as fast. She had a warm personality that was not hidden by her extreme intelligence. The dark circles around her eyes couldn't hide the compassion and concern she had for her patients.

She told me that even after seeing the pictures from the colonoscopies I'd had done throughout the years, she had seen cases of IBD that were almost as bad as mine that improved with a drug called Asacol. It was a drug with many properties similar to Sulfasalazine, and it was enclosed in time-released capsules designed especially for colonic disease. She said that we should give it a try as long as the biopsies they would do showed no cancer. At the same time, she cautioned me because there was still a chance that I had cancer.

This was not exactly what I wanted to hear. I don't know if I thought I would walk into Dr. Graham's office and she would tell me that there was no cancer and that I was cured of my Crohn's, but I still felt let down. All I heard was that there was still a chance that I had cancer, and it really started to hit home.

The tests were scheduled one after another, two weeks apart. There would be three in all, and the last one would be in early April. One would be a colonoscopy with many biopsies, another would be a barium x-ray, and the third would be an esophageal scope. All were painful and involved "prepping," which meant drinking Go-lytely and other fluids that clean out the digestive tract. The result is numerous trips to the bathroom, which was uncomfortable not only to my colon but also to my rectum, which was very tender and scarred.

For about eight weeks, all I did was stay in my bedroom and pout. I was sinking lower and lower. I slept for more than 12 hours a day; I wasn't working anywhere; I rarely exercised; I barely spoke to anyone. Thoughts about dying dominated my mind.

My parents obviously knew something was wrong. After all the fighting I had done to cope with the disease, I was fighting a losing battle. In the months prior to my last appointment with Dr. Thomas, I began giving myself enemas with a liquid drug called Rowasa, an anti-inflammatory drug used in severe cases of IBD. The only problem was that my colon was so inflamed that it regurgitated even the smallest amount of liquid that was poured into it.

Enemas are usually given when the tip of the bottle is inserted into the patient with the patient lying on his or her left side. Since the colon winds around the left side of the abdomen most people are able to hold it in for at least an hour and then expel what isn't absorbed. Every time I tried to do this, the medication flooded out all over my legs. It was a waste of time and a waste of the Depends that I wore to bed every night.

I knew that I needed to give this medicine a shot. The only way I could possibly keep the liquid inside me for an hour was to try to use gravity to my advantage. I began to rest upside down in a chair in my bedroom every night to give myself the enemas. I would lie with my head on the floor and my left side on the seat of the chair. My feet and legs were awkwardly draped over the back of the chair and braced against the wall. I did this for about 90 minutes every night. I was not going to give up without a fight. How heartbreaking it must have been for my parents to see me in this position.

I had been so active in the past and had gone all over the eastern part of the country playing baseball. Every night that there wasn't a game the following day, I had been out raising hell and partying somewhere. But at this time my world had been reduced to the 12'x12' space that was my bedroom.

I had basically severed all ties with my friends. I never called anyone, and my friends had figured out by then that I didn't want anyone to see me in this embarrassing state. I am not sure what people thought at those times in my life when I withdrew, and now it is really inconsequential. I do know that people were very guarded about asking questions related to my health on the rare occasions that I did interact with people. My company was limited to the terse conversations I had with my parents about my medications. My mother would come to my room crying and urging me to see a psychologist but I refused. I felt I was too tough for that, too. I just wanted to stay in my room and watch television.

I wasn't totally shut off from the world, though. Coincidentally, that was the same time that Mario Lemieux, the great Pittsburgh Penguins star, was diagnosed with Hodgkins' disease.

I had long been a fan of the Penguins. Even before they drafted Lemieux, I followed what was a perennial last-place team. Mario Lemieux changed that. For two years preceding his illness, he had led the Penguins to the Stanley Cup. He made the Penguins the toast of what had always been the Steelers' town.

Lemieux was my favorite athlete. He had a style and grace that hockey had never seen before in such a big man. The Penguins' poor records could not hide his brilliance.

Lemieux had much more adversity to overcome than just playing on bad teams. He had endured many injuries that rarely allowed him to perform at the elite level of which he was capable. It made me admire him all that much more. My favorite athlete and I were going through cancer scares at the same time.

It was a time when I had very little to look forward to in my life. Although I was only 26 years old, my future seemed so bleak. Even if the tests for cancer were negative it would set my recovery back and I would lose some weight. I would consequently lose a positive image of my physical self and set into motion the vicious cycle of my losing more self-esteem. The only thing I looked forward to was watching the Penguin games and the Mario Lemieux story.

When I was young, sports meant so much to me. As a kid, sports had provided me with many special moments, both as a fan and as a participant, with people who were close to me. I had recently regained the special feelings that sports can provide. It was becoming the only thing that stimulated my feelings and gave me a sense of anticipation. It was something to think about instead of worrying about whether or not I had cancer.

Even though all of the Pittsburgh media were giving constant updates on Lemieux, I still was in a little bit of emotional denial about my condition. I didn't allow myself to be too sad very often about my own plight. It is scary to even say the word "cancer" and your own name in the same sentence. There were such myriad emotions going through my head that they contributed to my physical exhaustion. I had suffered so many damaging blows that I felt punch drunk.

I remember watching the first news conference when Penguin officials and doctors made the announcement of Lemieux's diagnosis. It was very emotional for me. I didn't cry about my own problems. Yet when I saw a story about a hockey player I had never met, I broke down. It was like the Dave Dravecky story all over again.

# Chapter Ten

# I Knew How I Would Do It

## CHAPTER TEN — I KNEW HOW I WOULD DO IT

During that spring of 1993, I began to realize that I was starting to grow as a person. I was realizing how the experience was changing the way I thought about things. I was starting to feel emotions that I had suppressed all my life. Before then, I couldn't even humbly accept a compliment. I would accept nothing from others because I didn't want to owe anyone anything. Even though some of this self-realization was taking place, my self-image continued to plunge.

The thought of having cancer scared me when I permitted myself to think about it. The thought of not being able to return to normal activities until the tests were done depressed me. I replayed how humiliating those invasive tests had felt before. I felt I couldn't talk to anyone about the negative, pent-up emotions that I was experiencing. There was so much despair in me that I thought I might burst.

My mother continued to beg me to seek some psychological help. I stoutly refused. At least my ego would still be healthy. My mother and father could see the signs of depression in me. I was surly most of the time, and my thought processes were radical and paranoid. I would go through long periods of sleep, followed by even longer periods of sleeplessness. I would rarely bathe. I didn't care what I looked like. Life had a simple proposition: If the tests were negative, my life would go on. Probably not very well, but it would go on. If the tests were positive and I had cancer, I would end my own life.

I knew how I would do it—I would buy a gun. I always made sure that I had a few hundred dollars saved so I could afford to buy one. I knew who I would buy it from—there was a guy I went to school with who had all the connections for anything that was illegal or bad news. I knew where I would do it—in the woods behind my parents' house. There was a large space that opened up between there and the newly built highway extension for Route 22 that ran around the outskirts of Steubenville. I would do it there and no one would find my body for days. That way no one could save me if I only seriously injured myself.

As several weeks passed, I began to think about this every day in detail. It did not matter that the first test showed that there was no sign of cancer. There were still two painful tests to go, and I was still consumed with pessimism about the results. The steroids magnified the depression.

I had no appreciation for the things that I had. A great family that supported me through thick and thin and loved me unconditionally meant next to nothing. All the friends who called and expressed concern for me in the past years didn't make a bright spot on the blackness that had become my hardened soul. All the things that I had accomplished meant nothing.

During the time I had become ill, there were two young men from my hometown who died tragic deaths much before their time. These sad events didn't change my mode of self-pity at all. Although I often prayed for Paul Walkosky and Joe Prest, I didn't have any concern for the life I had that they no longer did. I was self-absorbed, childish, and stupid.

The second test came and went with no sign of cancer. I was relieved for the moment, but the greatest anxiety I felt came before the final test which was the most important—the colonoscopy. I had difficulty sleeping the two nights leading up to the eve of the test. On the night before the test, I just sat in the kitchen with my head in my hands.

My mother got up in the middle of the night to get a drink of water. I attacked her with many paranoid questions. She tried to reassure me that even if I did have cancer, I would be able to go on.

"What is going to happen to me, Mom?" I cried. "I'm going to have cancer and have to have that horrible operation."

"We will just have to see what the doctors say, honey," she replied.

It was typical of the way I acted. I was very selfish with my parents. I would go for days without speaking more than one-word answers to them and later go whining to them. I felt guilty about this, but I remembered the words a priest told me about it being a common dynamic of disease to lash out at those who were most supportive. I expected more out of myself, and this deepened my feelings of despair. Emotionally, I went up and down a lot.

Some days were not so bad. I would go through all the things in my head that I wanted to do, like going back to school, staying involved in baseball, having a family of my own, studying martial arts, finding a professional endeavor that was as gratifying to me and to others, and just flat-out becoming a better person.

Sometimes I would feel that these things were all within reach if I could just get a reprieve from the Crohn's. Then, I might possibly someday be able to understand the whole ordeal. I was trying to force myself to get better, trying everything I could possibly think of. The frustration was forcing me to open my eyes to other factors that might help my health. I started to think about my diet and wonder maybe if certain foods may have been exacerbating some of the symptoms.

I also began to believe that the mind could play a role in a human being's health. At night while I was resting upside down, I would meditate. I would envision the Rowasa enemas, which were a milky-white color, as a coating for my diseased colon. I would imagine it as cold ice cream pouring over red-hot coals. I would repeat the words "cool" and "heal" while imagining the fiery blood-red tissue of my digestive tract turning into the pinkish tone that healthy people have in their intestines.

Sometimes, I would be so deep in my concentration that I would fall asleep. Meditation can be like a sedative. The repetition of words or phrases in a quiet, consistent manner has a physiological calming effect on the human brain. It is the reason people have counted sheep for centuries in attempts to fall asleep.

People who are devoted to meditation and practice it properly and consistently experience many benefits. It is a stress reliever. Some people believe priests have longer life spans than lay people because of the extended amounts of time that they spend in deep prayer, which is very much like meditation. For many other people, it is an affirmation device that helps them believe in the hopes and dreams that they have for their lives. For me it was a frantic attempt to help save my life.

It was the first crack in the shield of my beliefs about my treatment. I was so hard-headed and stubborn that I could never be open to any ideas that were not mainstream. It was my ego again acting as a stumbling block, not only to my growth as a person and to my recovery from this horrible disease but also to my psychological and emotional battle to keep from taking my own life.

Taking medicine, or man-made pharmaceutical drugs, has been considered mainstream in Western society only for this most recent, comparatively small portion of the entire time that man has existed on earth. Before our "advances" in treatments for the things that ail us, home remedies, old wives' tales, and natural supplements were the only thing human beings had to ease pain. Human beings have become totally reliant on taking a pill for every little physical problem that crops up. It would be much easier to take a precautionary, preventative approach to our health care. It is better, as we are slowly learning to exercise, get proper rest, cope with stress properly, and, of course, eat right than to have to take medicine as a result of slothful behavior..

None of this even dawned on me until I had to use the enemas. It was about the same time that I read Norman Cousins' book, *Anatomy of an Illness*. My eyes started to open up to the possibilities of using supplemental therapies of many varieties.

Cousins wrote the book about his struggle with a degenerative, autoimmune disease that was destroying the connective tissue throughout his body. My mother had gathered a lot of books and information about support groups and new treatments, but I had always stubbornly ignored them. My back, at this time, was really against the proverbial wall when I decided to read Cousins' book.

There were some valid points Cousins made about illness and the way it is viewed by the person who is afflicted, by society, and by the medical community in general. Written in the late 70's, it was an eye-opener for many people in regards to the deity-like status that doctors often held in our society. It was a different perspective about how important the mind is to the healing of the body.

Cousins' book made me think that maybe other people felt the way I did, that disease can be as much emotional and psychological as well as physical. There was some substance to my thoughts about my mental state exacerbating my condition. The peaks and valleys that I was going through as I waited for the final results of the last test were every bit as excruciating as the physical pain that was being caused by the Crohns'.

When my mother and father drove me to the hospital for the last test, I had mixed emotions. One moment, I was begging God for another chance. The next, I was planning my own death. The dichotomy of sensations left me numb to most of the other things that were going on in the world.

I remained in that lost state when Dr. Graham told us that there was no evidence of cancer. The results came out negative. She did say it would take aggressive medicinal therapy to combat the ravages of the disease and that my chances for avoiding the surgery were slim. I didn't hear that part, however, because I was so emotionally spent by the whole process.

The aggressive approach to the medication involved increasing the dose of prednisone to 60 milligrams per day. It is an extremely high dose to be taken orally or even intravenously, for that matter. Dr. Graham and her medical staff were hoping that the large amount of steroids, combined with several vitamin supplements and the Asacol, would be the jolt my system needed to get the disease at least temporarily under control. Dr. Graham told me that I had never reached a state of remission from what she had seen in the review of my records. She was right. Once the disease got its grip on me, it just wouldn't let go.

As a result of the weight being lifted from me by the positive test results and the side effects from prednisone, my mood shifted 180 degrees again. I felt like I was on top of the world. Steroids gave me that illusion of invincibility.

I went back on my job search with renewed vigor. My good friend Matt Morrison had just taken over as head coach of our American Legion baseball program. He asked me if I wanted to help coach.

I wasn't sure at first. My lack of self-confidence told me that I hadn't done a very good job as a graduate assistant with Ohio U.'s baseball team. Working with two veteran, established coaches like Coach Carbone and Coach Toadvine made me feel inadequate even though I shouldn't have. The ego promotes competition with even those who are on the same side.

Another concern was the bathroom problem. I made up some phony excuse about being "too tired" to go on road games. I was always concerned that there wouldn't be a bathroom at some of our opponents' home fields like there was at our home field. Matt said he didn't mind and that I could just come to home games. I also became very interested in golf.

Golf gave me something to want to wake up for the next day. It allowed me to be out in the fresh air. It sparked my competitive juices and presented a challenege. It gave me a great deal of satisfaction, and it allowed me to enter into conversations with family, friends, and strangers. It forced me to be out in public, although it wasn't among large crowds of people.

It didn't matter that I was unemployed. It didn't matter that I had some things wrong with me. It didn't matter how much bad luck my life seemed to be filled with. All that mattered was being outside and hitting that little white ball.

I began learning to play fairly well. It gave me enjoyment to actually be good at something again. It also gave me a chance to join in social circles. My dad and my brother Tim also loved to play, and it gave me a chance to spend time with them.

Tim is the best golfer in the family. Although he is the smallest in physical stature, he hits the ball farther than all of us. I can remember sometimes when we were younger that I would say that he was too small to play with us. Since he was the best golfer, not only was he allowed to play, but he was also the first one asked to play. Many things turn around in life, and I am always happy to see this happen for my brother.

My dad and my brother also used golf as a way of expressing concern for me. My dad paid for a season pass at Red Oaks Golf Club in Bloomingdale, Ohio, just outside of Steubenville. Tim would come back from Columbus on the weekends to play. He gave me a hand-me-down set of clubs and other equipment. They always helped me with my game, and I knew they were looking out for me. There were a lot of good things that came out of my taking up golf.

It was also a distraction from the illness for me. I never had the panic attacks of having to rush to a bathroom while I was out on the course. My mind would be focused on things other than the pain and discomfort.

I think Matt Morrison knew this. Sure, he wanted me to help coach the legion team because I had something to offer. I think it concerned him and my other friends that I would rarely leave my parents' home. In addition to helping coach the team, I would also have a job taking care of the field.

It was also a good idea to have the job working at the field. It was another reason to be outdoors, keeping me active and my mind off my troubles. Vaccaro Field had been a source of great memories for me. Those memories had escaped my mind while I was so sick and depressed. Spending time at the field and reacquainting myself with all of the program's staff and support people who treated me like family made me feel good again.

Matt did a good job of surrounding himself with a very capable coaching staff. His father, Don "Butch" Morrison, helped him with the outfielders, scouting, and other duties. Bill Beattie, who was a standout player for the legion and West Liberty State College a few years before Matt and me, would coach third base. Matt was coaching the pitchers, and Mark Stacy was around helping the hitters.

Matt kept telling me he "needed" me to help. I know it was his way of helping me, trying to make me feel like I was important. He had more than enough coaching help, but he insisted that he needed me to help with the hitters and baserunners. It worked.

I didn't know what to expect. Matt told me he expected to have a really good team in another year or two but that he was unsure of his first team because they were so young. He felt that some of the new players needed to mature quickly for the team to be successful.

Success for Steubenville's American Legion team, of course, had to include the championship of eastern Ohio's tenth district. We had a streak of 18 straight years of winning the district title, but this year was going to be a big challenge. A couple of other teams were catching up to us talentwise. We didn't have a really dominant pitcher. Bob Sismondo was only 16 at the time and at least another year away from being a reliable, veteran stopper. We had another good lefty named Dan Corsi, but he was experiencing some arm problems, and we wondered how much of the load he would be able to carry.

Matt and I were worried that in his first year as head coach, we would be the first Steubenville team in nearly two decades not to make it out of the district tournament. We struggled to eventually win the title, and we were all relieved. Although eight of the 18 players on the team would eventually play Division I college baseball, that team was not especially strong. We were too young at that point.

It gave me a great deal of satisfaction to see that eight kids from Steubenville would eventually get the opportunity that I had received to play at the Division I level. The program now had that type of expectations. The kids believed they deserved success. It was probably the aspect of being involved with the program from which I derived the most satisfaction. I had maintained contacts with Division I coaches from my playing and coaching experience, and was able to call and alert them to the players that we had that were worth a look. Matt and the other coaches were very concerned about the players' futures, and we believed that it was as important, if not more important, than winning.

Being involved with the program helped restore some of my confidence. There is a special sense of pride that the people in the program have. There is a tremendous sense of confidence that we always had, and it meant a lot to me as a person and as an athlete. Being with the team again gave me another reason to feel good.

Sometimes the amount of prednisone I was taking made it very difficult to control my emotions. Sports can bring about some very emotional issues.

It was hard for me to keep my temper in tact, and I lost it a few times when people disagreed with me. Matt and I went at it, but we were like brothers who would beat each other up but always back each other up. I'm sure my temper was hard for people to understand. The wall I had so meticulously built around myself prevented people from knowing that I really wasn't like that at all.

The medication also gave me an extraordinary amount of energy. I would sleep for only a couple of hours. I ate constantly and I ate everything I could get down that was in my parents' refrigerator. I would lift weights in the mornings when I woke, work at the field, and golf in the afternoon. In the evenings, it was out to the baseball field for our games to end the day the best way I ever knew how.

Working on the field would normally be physically taxing for me, but prednisone was the great equalizer. I could rake, tamp, cut grass, clean up, line the field, and be ready for more, thanks to the steroids. It also allowed me to earn a little bit of money.

It turned into a great experience for me. Matt gave me a lot of freedom to teach the game. I started to feel that there was actually something meaningful that I was good at. Things were actually looking up.

# Chapter Eleven

# Leaping Before I Looked

# CHAPTER ELEVEN — LEAPING BEFORE I LOOKED

I received a lot of positive feedback about the work that I did with the legion team. I know that I helped some of the kids, and that gave me a rewarding feeling. I was never concerned about helping people before I became ill. It had always been about me first. People were suggesting to me that I consider a career in coaching and teaching.

My heart was still in pursuing a job in educational administration right away. The only problem was that I had no experience. I was still searching for jobs in educational administration, trying to use some of my father's contacts. I also looked into some of the doctoral programs in education administration at schools that were relatively close to Steubenville, like the University of Pittsburgh and Youngstown State University.

After summer of 1993 ended, I had a little time to catch my breath from the baseball season. Coaching had given me something to take my mind off my problems, but now that was over. I went back to work taking care of the field, and my job search continued, as did reflection on where my life was headed.

It was hard to believe that only several months before, I was ready to die at the age of 26. My prognosis was better but I was still hurting a lot. I had a desperate need to validate my existence through some kind of professional standing. I was addicted to the status I thought I had as an athlete. I was in competition with acquaintances, friends, family, and my past. My body was in better shape but my mind was still a mess.

As fall ended and winter approached, my work on the field ended. So did the golf season. I was still lifting weights but not much else. I sent out dozens of resumes. I had a few interviews but always finished runner-up. I didn't understand why God wouldn't have it in the plans for me to get one of these jobs, but in late December, I finally got a break.

An assistant baseball coaching position came open at West Liberty State College. It didn't pay much, but it was free room and board and great benefits including paying for doctoral work at West Virginia University.

The head baseball coach was Bo McConnaughy, who had been Matt's coach. Mark Stacy helped recommend me for the job. West Liberty President Clyde Campbell was a friend of my father's. I had a lot of good "ins" and they called me for an interview.

The position also included being a residence hall director in one of the dorms on campus. It was a place I was familiar with. I had raised a lot of hell when I would visit Matt, Maz Zrinyi, Danny DeLuca, and the rest of our friends who lived on campus during our college days. Danny's father affectionately called them the "hogs." It brought back many memories.

The interview went well. Coach McConnaughy and the administrators who took part in the process said they were very impressed with me. They called a few days after the interview to offer me the job.

I thought it over for two days. There really should have been no hesitation. I wasn't working at the time and I had few other prospects. My ego told me that I needed a job to help me feel better about myself. It would be a big help in that regard. It would also be something else to distract myself from the thoughts that were consuming me about my condition. But I began to worry about whether or not I would become sick again and have to leave the team. I worried about the bathroom situation in the dorm room and all the other concerns with the symptoms. I worried too much and talked myself out of accepting the position.

Fear overcame me again. The disease had an almost paralyzing effect on me psychologically and socially. I had mastered the art of excuse making to get out of commitments. I would say I was in too much pain or there was too much stress or it was uncomfortable or, of course, there was not a bathroom close by. I chickened out again.

Having to interact that closely with people was a huge concern. There would be times that I would have to sprint to a bathroom, and I didn't want anyone to see that. There would also be times, as there had been in the past, that a sprint to the bathroom wasn't fast enough. I surely didn't want anyone to see that. The disease was my crutch, my excuse, for sitting out of the game of life every time opportunity knocked.

I called Bo and told him that I would have to turn down the offer. He told me that he had a small amount of money for a part-time assistant coach. I wouldn't have to come every day, just enough times a week to work with the hitters. That was fine because West Liberty is only a 40-minute drive from my parents' home.

It was also a good way to keep my resume going. I had just missed out on a full-time job as an admissions counselor at the University of Pittsburgh. I couldn't understand why the only breaks I received were in baseball.

Craig Farrar also told me that he would like me to help out at my old high school when our season ended at West Liberty. He had just taken over as the head baseball coach and thought they had a chance to have a real good team that year. At least I would have plenty to do in the spring. Craig had coached baseball and football at Central when I played.

The experience at West Liberty did a lot for my self-confidence. I met a lot of other coaches and asked myself, "Why can't that be me?" I started to have aspirations of returning to coaching at the college level. It was the only area of my life in which I was actually gaining confidence. Fortunately, the symptoms of the disease were mostly quiescent that spring so I could concentrate on coaching.

After the successful season was over with West Liberty, I joined Central's team. I helped with the hitters and a few other duties. We had an exceptional group of kids. Seven of them went on to become Division I college athletes, an incredible number for what had become a very small high school.

The talent and the kids' attitudes carried us to the Ohio state baseball championship. It brought back a lot of memories. Nine years earlier, my classmates and I had played for the championship on the same field at Ohio State University's campus in Columbus, Ohio. It had been a full ten years since we had won the state American Legion crown.

The looks on the kids' faces after the win in the championship game gave me a great feeling. I remembered how proud I felt of our championship ten years before. I wanted to help the kids experience the pride and joy that comes from being successful at something that is worked so hard for. It was a special time, a fun time. It seemed like a lifetime since I had felt the same way.

That group of kids wasn't finished. Many of them were members of our legion team that had stormed through Ohio and won the state American Legion championship in August of that year. Many of the kids were being contacted by college baseball coaches. It gave me a chance to renew some of the contacts I had. Although I was starting to believe that I could be a college coach and starting to ask around the college baseball network about position openings, I had a few things that I needed to be concerned with if I was going to try to make a career out of college coaching.

Obviously, the first was my physical health. Would it hold up under the rigorous demands of college coaching? How about the travel and the problem of always struggling to find a bathroom? What about being able to exercise and maintain focus on healthy eating habits? Would I be able to travel and remember to take medication?

I discussed these problems with my parents, and they were full of encouragement and support, as usual. I remembered what Dr. Thomas had said about my being able to do whatever I wanted to do. I still felt restrained by the disease, though.

It wasn't just the disease that was restraining me from doing the things I wanted to do. It was me restraining myself. I was scared to do anything wrong or fail. Most of all, I feared others seeing me look bad. The real fear was exhibiting symptoms in public. I couldn't admit this to anyone and I desperately needed to find a way to cope with this fear. The fear depressed me. I continued to have big highs and small lows emotionally.

Early in the fall of '94, I finally acquiesced to my parents suggestions and the sensation that I was about to fall apart emotionally. I began to see a psychologist to try to cope with the feelings of depression and despair I had boiling deep inside me for so long. It was one of the toughest things about the illness. I had previously believed that anyone who even thought about seeking psychological help was weak or had horrible character flaws. It was another petty misunderstanding that I had in the distorted way I looked at things.

The therapy was helpful in many ways. It helped me realize that I had nothing to be ashamed of because I was sick. It helped me vent some of the pent-up anger I had been feeling. I was also able to examine my past failures and understand that fear of failure and the needless desire to be perfect kept me from getting the things I really wanted.

There was a lot of emotional pain involved in the therapy. I had to admit that I was very irritable and difficult to get along with, not only since I had been sick but before then, especially when I was drinking so much. I also confronted some of the problems my family had that I will always believe were partly my fault. I also realized that I was a has-been as an athlete. I wanted to coach, but I did not want to do it because I was trying to recapture my own glory days.

I didn't want baseball to be the only thing that I was ever good at. It was what I was best at, though, and where my heart was. I knew if I were ever going to be able to make an impact on people in a positive manner, it would be through baseball.

In late October of 1994, the disease flared up again. I fought it like a son-of-a-gun this time. I knew I had to increase the prednisone, which I did for a short period until the diarrhea came under control. When those symptoms became more manageable, the perirectal abscesses set in again.

The abscesses were especially vicious. I had searing pain most of the day and night, with the only relief coming from sitting on a heating pad or in the bathtub with the water as hot as could be humanly tolerated. My parents were probably sick of hearing the water running to fill the tub.

Sitting on the heating pad was flat-out stupid. Using a heating pad for prolonged periods of time is bad for several reasons. First, it can numb the area that is being treated, desensitizing nerves so that it is hard to feel how much heat is being put on the skin. Second, burns and damage to the skin can occur. It also provides only temporary relief.

I saw no other way to relieve the pain, though. The abscesses needed to be drained, and I was lucky that they found their way to the surface and were draining on their own. I could have suffered serious complications once again because I was reluctant to see a doctor. I was more determined than ever to conquer the disease, but I was also very bullheaded. Only by God's will did I not suffer any complications from the abscesses. I didn't realize at the time how lucky I was.

The abdominal pain and the abscesses were enough to leave me bedridden again. I would crawl to the bathtub three times a day and sit for a total of about five hours daily. The bathtub was a place where I could feel locked away from the world and my problems.

It was not much of a life I was living. When the disease was not flaring up on me, I was afraid to go anywhere for long periods of time because I still could not bring myself to go to the bathroom in public. When I was in a state of flare, I tried to stay within 20 feet of a bathroom.

As determined as I was to make something of my life, I was just as scared about having the colectomy performed. There were many thoughts that I believed at the time justified going through all of this physical, emotional, and psychological torture instead of having the surgery. Of course there was no guarantee that if I had the surgery, the same symptoms wouldn't appear in my small intestine. Then my life would still be miserable and I would have one less body part. If the abscesses spread and my life ended, so be it, I thought. What I wasn't realizing was that I had no life at the time, anyway.

I spent most of the fall of 1994 in my bed, on the toilet, and in the bathtub. I didn't lose as much weight as I had during the other flare-ups (about 30 pounds), so I kidded myself that this was a good sign. I told myself that I was learning how to manage the flare-ups better. In reality, it was worse because the flare-ups were emerging with more frequency.

I was in a state of panic trying to find something to distract myself from the suffering. I knew that anyone who would hire me as a college baseball coach would have to be very understanding about my condition. There might be times when I might not be able to even be on the job at all, and that was not good.

I called Coach Carbone late in the fall about a couple of jobs around the country. They didn't pay much because they were entry-level positions, but I needed a place to start. I had no luck even landing an interview. The urgency was a strong motivator.

I felt as though I had to have a job to have any self-esteem. Sometimes, insecurities serve as the best motivators. Many people who are successful permit this to serve as the driving force behind their high levels of ambition. It can be the ego searching for justification. It was exactly what I was thinking, only I hadn't experienced any professional success. My morbid thoughts were increasing again.

Just when it seemed that all avenues were closed and I may have to wait until college jobs came open again at the end of the spring, Coach Carbone called from OU. Two of his assistant coaches had left suddenly to take other jobs, leaving only Coach Toadvine and him to coach 35 players. He asked me if I would like to come back and revive my role as third coach on their staff.

I jumped at the chance. Although the finances were a little strained, it was a great opportunity for me at the time. It was also a big move. For once I leaped before I looked. I actually threw caution to the wind and didn't worry about the money, a second job, a place to live, the pain, finding bathrooms, or any of the negatives that I formerly would have permitted to roadblock an opportunity that presented itself to me.

The position was a slight elevation from my duties the first time around as graduate assistant coach. I would have more responsibilities, which was the experience I needed to become a more capable college coach. The salary was limited, so I would have to find another part-time job to supplement my income. I knew I could work out all of these details if the situation was what I wanted bad enough. It would be a long while before I started to believe this as an everyday philosophy.

I found a small apartment just outside of Athens that would be affordable on short notice if I could find another job. I wanted to avoid the bar scene because of the hours, the temptations, and the potential strain that the bar lifestyle might have on my health. I settled in during the first week of January and started back with the team as soon as I arrived.

It was good to feel a part of something again. There were a lot of familiar faces in the athletic department. There were also a lot of players on the team whom I had recruited and coached before. I thought this would be just what I needed to make me feel better physically and emotionally.

Practice was almost set to begin when I arrived. I would supplement my income through some small work-study type jobs that wouldn't interfere with practice and the other duties I had. Soon, however, those jobs dried up, and I was forced to find another source to help pay the bills.

Of course, I had friends who wanted to help me just as they had every step of the way. The DeLucas said that I could bartend at their place, and I was grateful for the opportunity. It would be the best thing that I could do to make extra money.

At first it worked out all right. Sometimes, I would bartend until two a.m., get to bed by three, and be back in the baseball office by eight. It didn't really register with me that I was running myself ragged. I had a lot of adrenaline going because I was so thankful and excited about the opportunity. I was also taking prednisone, which boosted my energy level.

I didn't really have time to think about my health. I was learning a lot from Coach Carbone and Coach Toadvine. I felt as though I could keep myself too busy for another bad thing to happen to me. In late January, just a few weeks after getting back on track, reality would force me to think about my health much more.

I had to drive to Steubenville on the day of the Super Bowl. We had a practice that morning, and I slept for a while after I went home. I was tired from bartending until three a.m. the night before. I finally started to drive to Steubenville when the game began.

Normally, I would never miss the Super Bowl. My priorities were changing. I knew that being a couch potato wouldn't get me any closer to what was becoming my dream of being a college head coach someday. It would certainly not help me fight Crohn's disease.

The drive to Steubenville made the trip to Pittsburgh shorter the next day. I had to see Dr. Graham on the day after Super Bowl XXIX. I always correlated events in my life chronologically with sporting events that were occurring simultaneously. I had not had a check-up in a while. Since the flare-up in the fall was minor, I didn't see Dr. Graham. It was another terrible mistake. Anyone who has a chronic condition needs to be in constant contact with a doctor, especially in times of crisis. I was stupid.

I was due for a colonoscopy. I was scared because I thought more damage might have been done to my colon since the last flare-up. If the pictures of my colon showed active disease or that more damage had been done, Dr. Graham might suggest surgery.

The anesthesia barely fazed me during the colonsocopy. My heart was racing and I was sweating. The test was painful, as usual. The air that is blown into the colon to widen it for the scope is very painful on a damaged organ. It became unbearable and I screamed like a baby.

After the test was finished I waited for Dr. Graham with my mother in one of the outpatient rooms. When she came in, she was not her normal, upbeat self. She was sullen, like many of the doctors I had seen who had delivered bad news to me in the past.

"These pictures are not good," she said. It was déjà vu from the time that Dr. Thomas talked with my parents and me before he suggested that I have the surgery.

"Your condition has not improved," Dr. Graham continued. "The medication is not working. There has been severe damage to this organ. It's definitely time for surgery."

"I'd rather die!" I exclaimed. The conversation was unpleasant. I was more arrogant than usual because I was under the influence of the anesthesia. I was too brave.

"It is your decision, but left untreated, there will only be more serious problems in the future," Dr. Graham said.

"What are the treatment options?" I asked. I knew what her answer would be.

"Colectomy," Dr. Graham replied.

I don't recall the rest of the conversation amongst Dr. Graham, my mother, and me. Every time I heard the word "colectomy," it was as though I went into a hypnotic trance. I would drift far away into another world at the sound. It was a world where I pictured myself dead.

Again, just when prospects were getting better for me, the disease would command more attention. I knew that the disease was getting worse but that no one could force me to have the surgery. The prednisone just masked the symptoms. I still had some hope, but probably at this time it had shriveled to smaller than the size of a grain of a mustard seed.

When I went back to Athens the next day, things were not all right. My attention span during our coaches' meetings was zero. Coach Carbone would give me things to do, and I would totally look right through him and not hear a word he said. People would order drinks from me while I was bartending, and I would forget what they said before I put my hand in the refrigerator less than ten feet away. I was consumed by this latest setback, both consciously and subconsciously.

I had always thought I could put on a brave face anytime I wanted to and act as though everything was fine. I thought I could lose myself in my work and activities and make myself better. This time was different. Dr. Graham was my last hope. I respected her opinion so much that I started to think that if she and Dr. Thomas said the same thing, the odds must have been insurmountable.

Still, I plugged on. I would get to sleep at 3 a.m., and be back in the office by eight. The effort I gave at both jobs was half-hearted. Fortunately, the DeLucas were very understanding about my work hours. It was a unique situation because their business was going so well at that point that they didn't get too worked up about someone missing work. In return, I gave them someone they could trust with their money. That part was working out well.

Baseball was a different story. We were picked in the 1995 pre-season to finish second in the Mid-American Conference. In March we suffered a few injuries, and several players had down years. Before we knew it we were hovering around the .500 mark. It was a big disappointment considering the expectations and the tradition Coach Carbone and Coach Toadvine had rebuilt.

Things were stressful and we hated losing. I would get frustrated with the tension, which is only natural when a team is losing. I would learn much more about these feelings later. Like any tense or uncomfortable situations that I had experienced in different times of my life, all I wanted to do was run away.

I volunteered to go recruiting all over the place. I went to different states and tournaments, all-star games, tryouts, and whatever other events in which potential recruits would be showcasing their talents. The driving was a great escape and more peaceful than having to worry about my problems. It was the experience that I hoped I would gain. As the season ended, it proved to be the most pleasurable of the duties.

In late June, my symptoms started to flare up again. I should have gone back to Dr. Graham, but I didn't feel comfortable with her at this point because she had recommended surgery the last time I had seen her.

A few weeks went by, and my condition was gradually deteriorating. I was doing some odd jobs, and we finished our baseball camp at OU in late June. I was spending a lot of time in the sun, and I would feel easily dehydrated. I was trying to sleep 12 hours a day, eat healthfully, and take the medication and vitamins, but it wasn't helping.

By mid-July, I was spending most of my time resting on the couch and feeling terrible. I still would not seek any medical help. I was as stubborn and stupid as I was sick. I was becoming depressed again and wishing I would die.

During the times that I would be so depressed, something invariably would give me some hope and inspiration to go on. As Dave Dravecky and Mario Lemieux had before, golfer John Daly provided me with some reason to think I might still have a chance.

Daly had burst into the nation's spotlight a few years earlier with his remarkable win at the PGA, one of golf's four yearly major events. People were in awe of how long he hit his drives, and tales of his off-the-course behavior began to near Ruthian proportion. Daly had admitted to having a drinking problem and was trying to keep it under control during the '95 British Open.

Daly conquered the weather, the course, some of the world's greatest golfers, and more important, some of his own demons to win the tournament in an exciting finish. It was a great comeback story, the kind I had grown to love. It was a happy ending like the one I was hoping I would have.

As I watched another sports figure overcome adversity to triumph, I realized that I must get some help. Like John Daly, I had a problem. I called my parents and told them things weren't going well. They were worried and insisted that I come back to their house.

I knew I was in trouble so I relented. I went back to my parents'

101

home in Steubenville, but I still refused to see a doctor. I was very angry that no one could find a calm for this horrible monster that seemed to rage inside me at will. I was taking my frustrations out on the medical community. I was not trusting anyone who had anything to do with modern medicine.

I was so frustrated about not being able to rid myself of the disease that I was grabbing at every straw I could. Just before I left Athens in late July, I made my first visit to a homeopathic doctor. Things that he said seemed to make sense, so I tried the remedy he prescribed. It did not help at all. He told me that if the disease was in an active stage, the remedy wouldn't work.

The flare-up was just beginning when I saw him. Would the remedy have worked if I had tried it at a different time? I will never know. The experience was another part of the journey I was on. At least my eyes were opening to the possibility of other treatments.

Years before I started experiencing symptoms, in August of 1984, as an American Legion baseball player and high-school football player, I had no idea that there was a time bomb ticking inside me.

I rarely allowed myself to be photographed while my Crohn's disease flared up. I had no choice but to pose for my Ohio University student identification card in the fall of 1989. I looked gaunt and frail with my parents a few months later during the holidays. My face was bloated and full of acne in the bottom picture with my brothers, Mark and Tim, at Christmas of 1992.

My family carried me while I was sick. Here, Mark and I give Dad a lift after he carried the Olympic Torch through Ashtabula, Ohio, in the summer of 1996.

I try to give back by doing things like playing baseball with children with IBD at Cleveland's Camp Superkids in 2001. Being active in sports means a lot for those kids, just as it did for my brothers and me in 1983.

Since my surgeries, all aspects of my life have been much more fun. Some friends and I are with Pittsburgh rock and roll icon Donnie Iris after a concert in Salem, Ohio, in August of 2001.

Steve Duco, my brother Mark, Dom Duco, Will Jenkins, Dad, and I celebrate at Will's wedding in Cleveland, Ohio, in June of 2001.

During two of my eight flare-ups with Crohn's, I was forced to go 15 consecutive days without eating even one bite of food because I was so sick. Now, I have at least two plates at most meals and eating is fun again. It wasn't much fun during flare-ups, like at my grandparents' 50th anniversary dinner in 1989 with Tim and my parents.

Whether I am demonstrating drills at practice, traveling to give a motivational speech (bottom left, opposite page, at the MaComb Co., Michigan, UOA Sept. 2004 meeting), lifting weights at home, or throwing batting practice to my players before a game, Coloplast products have helped me maintain my active lifestyle.

109

One thing that was always fun for me was baseball. I was so fired up for our 1998 team at Waynesburg College that I shaved my head before the start of the season. Our team did not disappoint. Here we are after winning the Presidents' Athletic Conference championship that year.

Our entire Youngstown State team stormed the field after defeating Cleveland State in the tournament's final game to win the Horizon League Championship on May 30, 2004, and I received a celebratory shower from Justin Thomas (2) and Frank Santore.

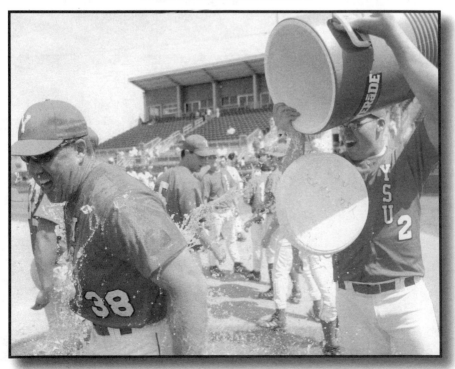

Our seniors proudly displayed the championship trophy, and I met with the media following our 2004 championship win. It was a much better feeling than displaying body parts and meeting with doctors.

I later hugged my mom, barely holding back tears of joy after many long struggles, and we knelt as a team in thankful prayer for our championship, while the scoreboard validated our faith in our dream.

We were honored to meet and play against the winningest D-I college coach of all time, Texas' Augie Garrido. Here we exchange lineups with the umpires before our June 4, 2004, NCAA regional game in Austin, Texas. The next week, I received the greatest honor of all when I became godfather to Elizabeth Mihalyo, daughter of my good friends, Mark and Amy Mihalyo, at St. Anthony's Church in Steubenville, Ohio.

# Chapter Twelve

# For a Reason

## CHAPTER TWELVE — FOR A REASON

Back at my parents' home, I was beyond miserable. I started to break down a lot. I was moodier than ever before. My thought pattern became darker than ever. I was becoming consumed with thoughts of death.

I again shut myself off from the world. I felt that I was too sick to even sit in a chair in front of a therapist for an hour. Therapists are for people who have some hope that things might get better. I had no hope, and I felt that no one could understand my pain and despair. I just wanted anything to make it go away. I don't know what stopped me from buying a gun. Perhaps it was because I was so sick that I couldn't leave my parents' house at all for several weeks.

I went back to lying on my head and administering medicated enemas twice daily, instead of just once. I spent upwards of four hours a day in the hot bathtub, which was another bad idea. I would perspire a lot, which would deplete me of the fluids I needed that were running out of me during my ten daily trips to the bathroom. I was in danger of becoming dehydrated.

It was hard to drink water to replenish the fluids that I lost. I would feel very bloated and have to run to the bathroom anytime I ingested anything. With all the senseless ways that I was trying to treat the illness myself, it's a wonder that I didn't incur much more damage than I suffered. The effort I was putting forth was dedicated but dangerously in vain. I desperately needed medical attention, but my stubbornness won out.

I felt everyone was against me. These feelings are symptomatic of anxiety disorders and/or depression. I ignored everyone and waited for any opportunity to lash out at my parents.

My father was understanding. He is trained in psychology and is a very well-read man. I know he spent plenty of time reading about the psychological ramifications of chronic illness concerning the patient and those surrounding the patient. He probably had a better understanding than most other people would have had.

He knew that I put more pressure on myself than anyone to get better. He was intuitive and perceptive enough to see by the way I looked and behaved whether I was doing well or poorly on a given day. He knew enough not to ask the rhetorical question, "How are you feeling?" It sometimes can make an ill person feel sicker to have to report the bad news every day. He would simply ask if there was anything I needed and give me support. Sometimes, I was too sick to even respond, but I know that he understood.

One day after he asked the question, I asked him if he had any books that I could read that might help my state of mind. It was a request that seemed to come out of my mouth with absolute spontaneity. I had not thought much about reading a book at the time. My concentration span was short because of the overwhelming fatigue and on-and-off bursts of pain that I would experience throughout my body. Nonetheless, the request just poured out of my mouth.

"How about this one?" my father said, reaching into a bookcase that he was standing in front of.

The book had a picture of a middle-aged man on the cover and the title read, *Your Sacred Self.* The author's name was Wayne Dyer. He looked like a normal, everyday guy that you might run into at a ballgame or a convenience store, but I would find out that he is not ordinary at all. I took the book from my father and sat it down on a tray in front of me.

Before my desperate state, I never would have thought about reading anything that implied such a spiritual concept. It would have shown a weakness in my character, or so I thought. I knew that I was very depressed and that the thoughts of blowing my brains out made me want to try anything. I didn't care if it compromised my ego at that point. I was searching to understand the purpose of my suffering.

As I half-heartedly thumbed my way through the beginning of the book, I began to doubt the usefulness of getting involved with the time it would take to read it. I was doubting the usefulness of everything, especially my existence. Then, as I turned to page 14, the words, in capital letters at the start of the next section, seemed as big as a brightly lit billboard on the side of an interstate highway: "YOU ARE HERE FOR A REASON."

You are here for a reason. You are here for a reason. At first, I just stared at the page and repeated these words over and over again. How could this pertain to me? Was this only for certain people reading the book? How could a sickly, depressed, bitter, nontrusting, washed-up, burden-to-my-family, lowlife like myself have a reason to be here? What was the reason? Was it to make others miserable? To make others sick?

My curiosity deepened. Would I really ever begin to understand why

I had to suffer so much? What about all the other unhappiness in my life?

I began to read the book, slowly at first. Then, I became enamored of every word. I read so voraciously that I didn't even think about my low energy level. I finished the book in one week. That is a quick pace for me, considering the book is 320 pages. Many of the ideas in the book made so much sense. There was indeed a reason for the suffering I was enduring, and although I didn't understand it at the time, I began to think that someday maybe I would.

Dr. Dyer wrote about the things that I really needed to think about, and the timing of my reading the book was uncanny. It was then that I realized that my ego was driving all my thoughts about worthlessness. It had done so my whole life.

The book also helped me realize that our bodies are nothing but the temples that house our souls. My body had been my main focus for so long, especially considering my involvement with sports. My soul however, was also diseased by all of the hatred and bitterness that I had kept inside me for so long. That hatred was fostered by my alcohol abuse and neglect of the things that should have been most important in my life: God and family.

In *Your Sacred Self,* Dr. Dyer writes that we all have equal worth on this earth as divine creatures created in God's likeness. There is no human being, fat or skinny, rich or poor, employed or jobless, black or white, healthy or sick, that is worth any more or any less in God's eyes.

This concept put a spike through my heart. I had always based my self-worth, and every other human being's, on tangible goals achieved or failed. They could have been physical, occupational, academic, athletic, or even alcoholic. I erroneously believed they had to be measured in some type of competition with other human beings. I had believed that my worth was high before because I was a better athlete and better drinker than many people I knew. When I became sick, I wrongly believed that my value had plummeted.

I was wrong all along. I would eventually come to know that God does not discriminate. I think that God loves us all equally and that is what truly matters. Dr. Dyer urges people to rid themselves of what he calls the "more-is-better" concept. It helped me to realize that my worth on earth was not based on anything I could achieve or acquire. It certainly was not based on the amount of physical gratification through alcohol and sex that was missing from my life now. I needed to release those old beliefs.

The book opened up a new way of thinking for me. I started to believe that practical measures could be taken to improve my outlook, which I had hoped would improve my physical condition. Maybe it wouldn't be such a radical concept for me to start watching my diet, to continue meditating, to take vitamins and supplements, to exercise when I felt up to it, or to get in touch with my spiritual being to help aid my physical being. I had thought about these things before, but I never believed them.

Another concept in the book was about "beliefs" and "knowings." Dr. Dyer basically describes a belief as something we think to be true; he describes a knowing as something we are certain is true. I began to have a knowing that all of these other conditions and circumstances were effecting my health. I knew that I had control over my diet, taking the medication religiously, meditating and praying regularly, exercising, and avoiding stressful situations as much as possible. I knew these things could help.

What I did not know was that God had other plans for me. I still didn't understand or want to accept the fact that I might have to live with an ostomy if I ever wanted to have a quality life. I wanted control over that. My determination, or stubbornness, grew. I would do anything to avoid the surgery no matter what the financial, emotional, or practical costs were. I was still dead set on being as ordinary as possible, even if it took extraordinary measures.

One of the extraordinary measures that I decided to pursue was attending a health care convention for which my mother had seen an advertisement in the *Pittsburgh Post-Gazette*. At the convention were many health care practitioners especially those of the alternative medicine variety. One of the people who especially caught my interest was Dr. Martin Gallagher, who specialized as a chiropractor and nutritionist.

Dr. Gallagher had many intriguing theories that seemed to make a lot of sense. He spoke of the state of the health care field, and about the fact that many people try to treat ailments with a quick fix in the form of prescribed pills. He noted that many of those people are later treated for side effects that are caused by the first medication.

He also spoke of the importance of watching one's diet carefully. He promoted a healthy diet, which omitted red meats, dairy products, foods with preservatives, and sugar, especially the artificial types. For the first time I began to understand that bread and all bread products contain refined sugars that are also bad, especially in excess.

The psychological and spiritual state of the patient was also important to Dr. Gallagher. He stressed that there was a very important mind-body connection. It was basically all of the things I had wanted to hear from a doctor for the previous seven years. It seemed that there was a direct correlation between my negative self-image and how terrible I felt physically.

These principles had also been discussed by Dr. Dyer. I started to become more aware of people who were professionally, financially, socially, and emotionally in good standing; they all seemed to be in good physical shape. Even when I was an athlete, I was not nearly in the physical condition I should have been in because of my partying. If I had eaten like a normal man, I would have weighed over 250 pounds with the calories from all of the beer added in.

Another principle Dr. Dyer wrote about was being able to observe your body. Your body will tell you when it needs sleep, exercise, food, drink, sex, or any other functions that we tend to abuse. I never understood this before. I lived and breathed the "more-is-better" concept. The more I read Dr. Dyer's book, the more it seemed like I was figuring out what I needed to do to help myself instead of waiting for a doctor to do something.

I was engrossed in Dr. Dyer's wisdom. As my health finally improved, I started to be able to get around again. I yearned for more from Wayne Dyer. I bought a couple more of his books, *Real Magic*, *Pulling Your Own Strings*, and *You'll See It When You Believe It*. I became fascinated by how peaceful, confident, reassuring, and loving his ideas were. Many of his thoughts were the things I never had in my life.

As I healed, I started to work out again and gain weight. It was obvious that I wouldn't have time to be able to fully recover and resume my coaching duties at Ohio U. I called Coach Carbone and told him that I believed that I had let him down. He reassured me that it wasn't a problem and that they would be okay with it.

I knew I had to go back to Athens. There were more than three months left on the lease for the apartment I was renting, and I also had a few job opportunities there. The DeLucas offered to have me back at the bar, which was kind of them.

There was another opportunity, however, that captured my interest. Stan Sanders, the former baseball coach at the University of Toledo, became an entrepreneur after he left coaching. He had a patent on an idea for placing maps in hotels around particular cities that would locate area business. He needed sales reps to make representations to local businesses. Coach Sanders was an assistant at Ohio U. under Coach Wren, and he had coached Joe Carbone and Bill Toadvine. I called him and asked him if I could take on the project.

I felt comfortable trying this in Athens. There were some local businessmen I knew that I thought might have some interest. I was gaining more confidence in myself after overcoming each flare-up. Little things didn't matter as much to me as they had before. I started to care less about what people thought. There was the obvious motivation to make money. Another plus was that the project would last for only a few weeks and be over with. It was also a challenge because I had to do something that I was never good at—initiating a first meeting with strangers.

I went to every business in the town that I thought might be a prospective customer. I tried to make my appearance and presentation as professional as possible. I hustled for about ten hours every day. The latest flare-up was still ending at the time, so occasionally I would have to sprint to a bathroom. Sometimes I didn't make it in time. I did not let this deter my enthusiasm. It was a project that I had high personal stakes in.

After a few weeks of selling ads, I had accumulated enough customers to fill Coach Sanders' quota. I also had enough to make a few thousand dollars for myself. The project was renewable yearly, so it would be easy to do again.

Just when I thought I had really done something good, one of the larger hotels in the area withdrew its support of the project. It would not have been fair to the local businesses to continue without the hotel. I went to some of the local businesses and gave back checks to those who had made early deposits. I was discouraged, to say the least.

I had worked hard and success had seemed imminent. The rug was pulled out from under me. I asked God over and over why this always seemed to happen. I could find no answer.

Had the project been a success in a rural town like Athens, I surely would have taken it to larger cities with more hotels and businesses. I had enjoyed the work despite the fact that I was too physically exhausted at the end of the day to do anything but read some Wayne Dyer and pour some enemas into my rear end. I would not be able to waste another month without a paycheck.

I was still unsure about a future in coaching. The most recent flare-up was a big blow to the assurance I had that I could handle the stress. I was set to move back in with my parents, and I had no idea what would happen.

I kept telling myself that everything was happening for a reason, but I was ashamed of myself because it seemed that nothing was going my way. I knew that Dr. Dyer was correct when he wrote that everyone has a purpose. I started to wonder if my destiny was to be a washed-up ex-jock who was sick all the time.

Having surgery was the prudent thing to do. I saw Dr. Graham again, and she arranged a meeting with a staff surgeon, but after the meeting, I was even more bullheaded about having the colectomy. I talked with the surgeon again only to appease my parents and Dr. Graham. The surgeon admitted that the surgery could be emotionally traumatic. Many surgical professionals equate the sentiment to that of losing a limb.

"Have we made any progress with you as far as having the surgery?" Dr. Graham asked.

"No," I flatly replied.

"I am certain that we have expired all medical options and that surgery is your only hope for leading a normal life again," she said.

"What about the other dangers, like cancer or other problems setting in?" my mother asked.

"Those possibilities are endless," Dr. Graham said.

I acted like a baby. "It is easy for you people to say. It is not your body or your life," I said. "I mean it, I would rather die."

"What will it take for you to realize the dangers?" Dr. Graham asked. "There are many emergency situations that could arise."

"Then that is exactly what it will take, an emergency situation," I replied.

This was another example of just how supportive my parents were. They could have given up on me, but they didn't. They were just quiet and supportive, just like the time that my mother drove two hours round trip for 35 consecutive days to see me the first time I was admitted to Allegeheny General, or the time when my dad slept on the floor of my hospital room in the Cleveland Clinic and ran a college while attending to my needs.

I don't know how much more of an emergency situation I could have put myself in. That's right; I put myself in the situation. Instead of facing the problem that was before me, I was running from it. I would not be a gracious loser because losing to me meant death, and it would be death by my own hand.

I had come to understand many things during this flare-up. I understood that God had provided human beings with the capability to achieve almost anything within their reasonable desires. I understood that I could help my situation by focusing on positive thoughts and taking measures like diet maintenance, exercise, rest, and natural supplements. I also know that God has a plan for each one of us, and that I could do anything I set my mind to. The variable in the equation was God's plan for me. I could not accept having the surgery.

The dichotomy of thought patterns was astounding. On one hand, I felt such optimism and empowerment that I thought I might burst. Conversely, I was solemn about my vow to kill myself if my condition worsened to the point of that "emergency situation" necessitating surgery. The range of emotions was compounded by the high dose of steroids I was taking. It was downright scary. I thought I was going mad. I would go sometimes to the spot where I planned to shoot myself.

I would scream at the top of my lungs. The woods were secluded enough that no one in the surrounding residential areas would hear me. Other times, I would sit peacefully and be amazed at the wonder of the tranquil wilderness that God created. I would really feel God's presence and tell myself that I never wanted to leave the world.

Those screaming times, though, were filled with evil. When you think about harming anyone, including yourself, it is flat-out evil. Probably the greatest tragedy was that I understood more things than ever, but I was regressing as a person because I was not acting on that knowledge. I didn't appreciate the future I had ahead of me, which those who I knew who had left this world too early would never experience.

Although finding a job would help alleviate my emotional pain only on the surface, I still felt it was the thing I most needed. I knew that I had talents and that God had a plan for me, but maybe that plan was for me to die young. I didn't realize it then but I had a little more ambition than to just die at age 28, and I just needed to catch a break somehow.

# Chapter Thirteen

# Or Was It Luck?

# CHAPTER THIRTEEN — OR WAS IT LUCK?

Wayne Dyer writes in several of his books that if we have faith and are on our proper path, God will send the right people, vehicles and opportunities into our lives at the right times. I have found this to be incredibly true. This was especially evidenced in my life in late 1995.

Dave Walkosky, Paul's brother, had just been named assistant football coach and head baseball coach at Waynesburg College in Waynesburg, Pennsylvania. It is a small, NCAA Division III college, and its campus is located right off interstate Route 79, one hour south of Pittsburgh and a half hour north of Morgantown, West Virginia.

Dave had just finished his masters' degree and graduate assistantship at Memphis State University. He had an outstanding career as a defensive back at the University of Toledo. Baseball was not his forte though, and he was thinking about having his brother Mike be his only assistant coach. Mike had been a great athlete and a fine baseball player in his own right. He also had some coaching experience, but he was involved in several businesses in Steubenville, which was a 70-minute drive from Waynesburg. It would be difficult for him, to say the least.

Our families were good friends; the four Walkosky boys and the three Florak boys were all close in age. We all participated in sports and were teammates and friends. I had coached with Mike in 1994 at our high school when we won the state championship. When I was in town, I would look Mike up. One day he told me that Dave needed some help.

I had been mulling over whether or not to continue coaching. I erroneously believed I was managing the flare-ups better, but the disease was really preventing me from sustaining anything. I was still thinking about pursuing a doctorate in education because I thought it might be a bit easier on me physically. I had some part-time work in Steubenville but nothing to hang my hat on. It seemed like baseball was a pipe dream for me, especially with my health concerns. Now, however, the right vehicle and circumstances were being put in my path.

After talking with Dave, I thought it would be a good thing for me to do. He was the right person showing up at the right time. Basically, he wanted me to run the show on the field. I would call all of the pitches, set the defense, and coach third base. Those are almost all of the major duties that baseball coaches can have at that level during a game.

Dave also told me not to worry about being there for practices every day. That was a good thing because almost three hours in the car every day would have been tough, considering how fragile my health was at the time. I would make only a couple thousand dollars, but the experience would be great. As Christmas approached, I was back in with my parents in Steubenville. It wasn't where I wanted to be, but it was the place I was supposed to be at the time.

As the New Year turned, baseball teams were beginning to get ready for the 1996 season. We had to start with that year's edition of the Waynesburg College baseball team. The first day of practice, I thought that this was anything but the right place at the right time. We practiced in the college's old gym that was small and beginning to become run-down. There was only one old batting cage. The players had no practice uniforms, and their skill level was much different form the players I had coached the previous year at Ohio U. People walked in and out of the gym at will, and we continuously had to halt practice to let them through.

I was amazed; it was not nearly the serious, controlled atmosphere I was used to. When Dave and I talked, many of the kids had empty looks in their eyes as though they did not believe what we said. They had been used to a more laid-back approach when we arrived. Dave and I were anything but laid-back. We both had a lot of Coach Bahen in us. I think some of the difficulty we had in those first few days had to do with our high expectations, plus a little of the usual players-getting-used-to-new-coaches thing.

It was evident early on that we did not have a wealth of talent. I didn't know what to expect from Division III competition, but I still knew that we would have to drill fundamentals as often and as quickly as possible. Our first game was scheduled for Cocoa Beach, Florida, in six weeks.

Another guy helping out as an assistant coach was Richard Krause, a professor in the English department at the college. He taught mostly communication classes that were encompassed under the school's English program. He was from nearby Carmichaels, Pennsylvania, and was baseball fanatic. He was well-connected in baseball circles throughout the area and knew the game well.

It just so happened that an employee at the college had left at the beginning of the semester. That individual was teaching one of the communication courses about the profession of sports communication and management. When the English department began its search for a replacement instructor, Richard was a natural liaison between the administration and me. It seemed that this journey to this small, Midwestern college town was full of great strokes of luck. Or was it luck?

I had the qualifications that were necessary, a master's degree and teaching experience from substituting several times when I was in Athens in 1995. Plus, sports communication was right up my alley. Again, another instance of the right things coming my way at the right time.

I was a little nervous at the beginning of the course, but things went pretty well. I spent a lot of time preparing lectures and trying to keep the students enthusiastic. It was just enough for me at the time to teach one three-hour course and be at baseball practices every Monday, Wednesday, and Friday.

In mid-January, my grandfather died. His condition had been steadily declining the preceding few years, and he was bedridden most of the time. It was hard on my mother, not only to see her father struggling to retain his dignity while dying a slow death but also to drive to Pittsburgh more than several times a week to make sure he was being taken care of.

His death was sad for all of our whole family. He was loved dearly and was our elder statesman. It had an effect on me because I held most of the emotion in. On the inside I was very sad.

I'm sure it was a negative factor in the state of my health. A short time after the funeral, I began to experience the usual flare-up symptoms. I thought I would be in big trouble again. Fortunately, it would not end up being as severe of a flare-up this time. Still, I could only sit at the desk in the classroom when I lectured. Standing was too painful. Practices were not easy, either. I did not even dream of throwing batting practice because I knew I would be overwhelmed with pain.

I was desperately searching for answers. I thought it was time to seek the opinion of another expert. I made an appointment to see Dr. Gallagher, the chiropractor whom my mother and I had seen at the Health Expo.

It was a different experience as far as health care treatment is concerned. There were many people dressed in white outfits, as is customary in an M.D.'s office. There were a receptionist and a waiting room filled with chairs, coffee tables, and magazines, the usual stuff. That is where the similarities ended.

I was called in to see Dr. Gallagher right on time. He was friendly and very personable, and he asked me many questions. Some were about my physical symptoms. Other questions were about my diet. It was as thorough as an exam as I had ever been through.

Dr. Gallagher's plan was to have me eliminate things from my diet that were building up toxins and possibly creating allergic reactions in my colon, and possibly other organs. I would have to keep track of everything I ate at every meal every day for one month.

It was hard and I had to be very committed, but I knew it had to be done. I was losing weight and energy, but I felt mentally recharged by having such a featured role on the coaching staff of the Waynesburg College baseball team. It was the only thing that kept me fighting the flare-up.

The teaching was also exciting. I tried to keep current on sports news. This was a good thing, too, because it made me read a newspaper every day. I gave the students current events quizzes in the world of sports to make sure they were keeping up. I tried to make reference in my lectures to current events for much of the time that we were in class. The challenge was making me feel like a well-rounded person. Seeing Dr. Gallagher made me well-rounded as a patient, or so I thought.

My condition continued to aggravate and frustrate me. I knew that I was doing a good job teaching and coaching, but I thought I would be much better if I were healthier. Even though my eyes were opening to new ways of thinking, the same depressive thoughts would creep in. I wondered even if the meticulous work that Dr. Gallagher and his staff did could keep me from these nasty flare-ups. I had no social life at all, and I would sleep for 12 hours on my days off, trying to recharge my body.

The bathroom was my constant companion again, seven to ten times per day. A typical day went like this: Wake up, go to the bathroom. Shower, have a little bit to eat, and go to the bathroom again. Then I would make the 70-minute drive to Waynesburg, hoping that I wouldn't have to go to the bathroom again until I arrived on campus. There is a stretch on Route 79 to Waynesburg in which there is very little civilization, and no place for a bathroom emergency. Many of the rides were filled with fear. Fortunately I never had an accident, either with my bowels or the car, but the trips were more tense than they should have been.

After I would arrive on campus, I would quickly find a bathroom then go to the classroom to teach the class for an hour. Sometimes I would have to leave in the middle of my lecture to sprint to the bathroom. Then I would talk with Dave about our practice schedule and go to the bathroom after lunch again. Then we would start practice, and sometimes I would have to leave the gym to go again.

When practice was over, I just felt relieved to make it through the day without losing control over my bowels. I felt as though I had won a small victory every day if I could do that. These challenges were not as big as the ones that were ahead, though. We would have to travel on spring trip on a plane flight that would take nearly three hours. If there was someone in the plane's bathroom when I needed to go, I would be out of luck.

Also, I knew that finding a bathroom at some of the ballparks we were playing in might be tough. Most of the fields we could play on would not be as contemporary as the Division I opponents we had at Ohio University. They would either have very run-down bathrooms or none at all. I was, however, finally conquering my fear of going to the bathroom in public.

As early March approached, I was about 50-50 on the chance of even making the trip to Florida with the team. I was feeling worse. I knew that the team and Dave needed me there. Plus, I would room with Richard, which would make it easier. He is a very easygoing, understanding person. He also explained that I had nothing to be embarrassed about because there were instances of IBD in his family. He knew what the disease was all about. It was important for me to know that if I had to share a hotel room with someone for a week that he wouldn't be freaked out by the symptoms. I decided not to let the disease stop me. We flew out of Pittsburgh on the first Friday in March.

The flight went off without incident, and I made it all the way to the hotel in one piece, although I was wiped out. It rained hard the first day and all of the fields were filled with water, so the games were cancelled for the first day. While I was sitting around the hotel room, I felt a lump at the front of my rectum that was getting near my scrotum. I knew it was an abscess, and I knew I was in no-man's land because it would be at least a week before I could get back to Pittsburgh to see Dr. Graham or get any of the proper medications.

I sat in the bathtub for about two-and-a-half hours that night, hoping that it would somehow drain out. Because of the size of the lump I thought it had a good chance of finding its way through the skin and the outermost epidermal layers quickly. I didn't think about it getting into my bloodstream. I was being foolish, trying to treat an abscess on my own.

Before the game the next morning, I sat in the hot bath for an hour. Still no results. We went to the field, and I was having a great deal of discomfort. We had batting practice in the small cages outside of the fields at the complex. There were three cages and three coaches. That meant Richard, Dave, and I would all have to throw batting practice.

When I first started throwing, taking a stride every time to throw made me wince in pain. There was a lot of pressure in my backside and it felt like there was an anchor in my butt that was ready to bottom out. After I pitched to three hitters, I suddenly felt great relief. I stepped outside the cage and around the corner, and I undid my uniform pants. There was a huge pool of blood inside!

At first I was scared, but then I realized that the abscess had indeed found its way through the skin. I had temporarily dodged another bullet. It wasn't the first time that the sight of blood gave me a sense of relief.

About six months before, during the flare-up I had in the previous September, blood coming out of me was a good sight. It was right after the last flare-up that caused me to leave Ohio U. I had been experiencing heavy lower abdominal cramping toward the end of the flare-up. One day while I was sitting in the bathtub, my abdomen started to spasm on the lower left side. Suddenly, a huge blood clot, about seven inches long and four inches wide popped out of my rectum. It was about an inch thick, and the shape of a football. It was bluish-red in color, and felt almost like Jell-o, only with much more consistency.

I was ready to scream but I felt relieved. It was not really good to have a blood clot that size come out of my colon, but it made me feel physically better. Under the circumstances I should have sought immediate medical attention, but I wasn't really under the care of any doctors then. Who knows what could have happened if God wasn't watching out for me?

Six months later in Florida, God was still watching out for me. I turned to go back in the cage, bloody pants and all, and resumed throwing as if nothing happened. Some of that was strong will, and some of that was stupidity. We finished batting practice, and we played the first game and lost, 3-2. It was so good to be out there. It was a night

131

game under the lights. The weather was good and the atmosphere was great. It was my first time giving the signs and making all the decisions from the third base coaches' box. I felt good but I made a few mistakes. Some of that was just from adrenaline. I felt nervous with a sensation of anticipation that I had not felt in a long time. I knew that I was doing what I was supposed to do.

We were mediocre at best the rest of the trip, although we did beat Bridgewater, 6-2. They would go on to play in the Division III World Series that year. The trip was not very enjoyable for me because of my health. Twice I had to leave in the middle of a game to rush to a bathroom. Once I had to get in one of the team's vans, which was parked all the way behind the outfield fence and drive to the nearest bathroom at a McDonalds' which was a half-mile away from the field. I missed an inning-and-a-half. Another time, I didn't make it and simply missed the last inning of the game cleaning up my clothes and the mess in the bathroom. It was a lopsided game anyway, but the condition was very much affecting my work. I tried to put on a brave face as I walked back to the dugout.

"Hey, are you all right?" Dave asked with a look of disbelief on his face.

"Yeah. It happens sometimes. Don't worry," I shrugged.

I don't know what Dave really thought, or if anyone involved with the team knew that there was something very wrong with me. I wasn't really trying to be tough; I was more embarrassed than anything. It was a distraction for me. I wanted my mind to be on my job, not on cleaning things up. I was used to the pain and the discomfort. It had become a part of my every day routine, right up there with brushing my teeth, taking a shower, eating, and sleeping. Pain was a constant companion.

I was ready for the trip to end. The team didn't really embarrass itself as bad as I thought we might. We won three out of eight games. I thought we had the potential to do a lot worse. I had a sense of satisfaction because I finally felt that I really had made a difference and that I was needed.

The flight home was good. I finally felt relaxed. The day before we came home we stayed in Orlando. Most of the team went to Disney World, but I just stayed in the hotel room and slept. I always tried to make sure I was getting plenty of rest, even during the times that I didn't feel too bad.

When I got home, I made an appointment to see Dr. Gallagher again. I was fortunate that I didn't have to be on a special diet during the trip because we ate almost exclusively fast food. It is a little easier to eat a healthy diet when eating a fast food diet now than it was in the past. They all have salads, and many of them have grilled chicken and baked potatoes on their menus.

I was noticing that when I tried to eat healthfully, my symptoms were not as severe. It is so hard, however, to eat right when you are on the go all the time. That is the reality of being a college coach. You get a lot of fast food, packed luncheon meats and soft drinks. It seemed as though the soft drinks made me feel worse than anything.

When I went for my appointment with Dr. Gallagher, I learned that I would have to start paying a lot more attention to the foods that I ate and the effects that they might be having on me.

He looked at the record of the foods that I had been eating. I didn't think I was doing too badly with my diet, but Dr. Gallagher had different thoughts. There were many things he told me to eliminate. He also prescribed many supplements for me that would help improve my condition.

It was a revelation to me. I thought that many of the breads and pastas that I had been eating were good for me. Dr. Gallagher explained that I may be allergic to wheat, causing many of the inflammatory reactions I was having with my skin, joints, sinuses, and digestive tract. The allergy theory made sense because I was having reactions in more than one membrane.

Those bread products contain unrefined sugar, which is terrible for human beings to ingest, according to many nutritionists. It is one of the leading causes of obesity, as well as many other medical conditions.

Dairy products and red meat were out, as well as any processed foods. Most of my diet would be excluded. It would be a big change in my lifestyle and would take much sacrifice and dedication.

The diet was hard to stick to during the second half of the season. We were traveling to some of the games, and I would spend more than 12 hours with class and the team some of those days. In the modern diet of the Western world that is loaded with bread, dairy, meat, sugar, and pre-prepared products, one or more of these products appears in almost every food one may choose. I had chosen my meals out of convenience and not by nutritional value.

The team did better than I anticipated. We finished with a .500 record, not great by any standards but miles ahead of where I thought we would be after our first practice. I really believed that I contributed a lot. I made most of the on-the-field decisions, and I became more involved in recruiting. I also wrote several articles on various subjects that appeared in different newspapers in the area.

With the writing, the teaching, and the coaching, I was finally gaining valuable experience. I really enjoyed the work, and I knew this would be a good stepping stone for my career. The situation as a part-time employee was not one that I would seem to be able to stay in for a long time. I was tired of seeing my parents pay my medical bills, but there were many things that I liked about Waynesburg College.

The college was so close to home. It was also only one hour from Pittsburgh, where all my doctors and other health care practitioners were located. My father and I still went to the Steeler games, which was a nice outlet for him from his job pressures and for me from my health problem. I had a very good relationship with Richard, who was emerging as a leader amongst the faculty on campus. I also got along very well with Rudy Marisa, our athletic director, and, of course, Dave Walkosky. I also thought that despite the challenges the baseball program faced, we could win there. I wanted to stay.

When the school year and the season ended, I told Richard and Rudy that I would somehow like to stay. They said they would do anything they could, but they wouldn't promise me anything. The staffs at small colleges are very limited, and people are expected to have two, sometimes three, positions to be considered for full-time employment. I was preparing myself for this with the baseball, the teaching, the writing, and some of the work that Dave let me do in the sports information office. I knew I could stay on and at least do the same things I had done, but I knew I would need an increased workload or something on the side to make more money.

# Chapter Fourteen

# A Regrettably Familiar Role

# CHAPTER FOURTEEN — A REGRETTABLY FAMILIAR ROLE

One of Wayne Dyer's principles is to do what you are good at and pursue it with passion, and the necessary money will follow. I was living this belief and not knowing it. I loved baseball. I loved teaching the game and being able to make a positive impact on young people's lives. I loved the competition and the rush that I felt when one of our players executed something I taught.

The necessary money was there. Although my parents were paying my medical bills, I had enough to cover everyday living expenses. The thought of being 28 years old and still living in my parents' home didn't sit well with me, but it was where I had to be at that stage of God's plan.

As the summer of 1996 approached, I set out to find another job that would give me flexibility so I could still retain my duties at Waynesburg. I was helping to take care of Vaccaro Field and doing a lot of golfing. I was trying to follow Dr. Gallagher's diet and having a tough time.

I found out that socializing was extremely hard while staying on the special diet. When human beings gather for a social event, there is almost always some type of eating and drinking going on. Even tap water was prohibited on the diet, and I hated being faced with temptation so I didn't socialize at all. I even skipped a couple of friends' weddings because I didn't think that there would be anything on the menus that would be agreeable to the diet.

In early August, my mother decided to have both of her knees replaced. She had fought a long battle with arthritis, and it was becoming painful for her to move around. It had been a difficult few years for her. With my being in and out of the hospital and attending to my special needs in addition to her secretarial work, she had some heavy burdens to bear. In addition to witnessing her father's slow, agonizing death, she watched my father undergo successful surgery for prostate cancer in the spring of '95. There were plenty of stressful trips to hospitals and painful images of people she loved having to suffer. The stress exacerbated her condition, and after a long period of struggling with pain and discomfort, she scheduled surgery for early August.

Although my mother had become much stronger about seeing loved ones in pain, I was weak. When she woke up after the surgery, my dad, my brothers, and I were there. The image will always be strong in my mind of the pained expression she wore on her face when the nurses came in to flex her knees shortly after she woke up.

I wasn't prepared for my reaction. I had always feared seeing people with physical maladies. I had started to grow out of it, and the fear was not nearly as bad as it was when I was a kid. If I saw someone in a wheelchair, or missing a limb, or on an oxygen tank, I would get a terrible sinking feeling in the pit of my stomach. I turned and ran from these situations. The situation with my mom had to be different. It pained me to see someone I loved so much in so much pain. I had a physical feeling of sickness in my stomach that was real and not imaginary when I walked in to see her.

She was the one who had been by my side through my whole ordeal. She was like a rock for me. I needed to fight my weakness to be there for her. I fought back tears and stayed in her room until it was time to leave.

For the next two weeks, I vowed to be there every day, just as she had been for me. She had made the drive to Allegheny General every day for each of the 35 days I was hospitalized when I was first stricken with the symptoms. It was over a two-hour round trip every day that showed much dedication and love on her part. My ego foolishly told me that I needed to compete with her and pay her back. I realized that families do those things for each other, but I believed that I owed it to her to be there every day.

I didn't handle the situation as well as I had hoped. Her room was on a rehabilitation floor, and there were many patients with various physical maladies that I saw every day. The sinking feeling came to my abdomen many times in those two weeks, and my appetite and energy level began to wane a bit.

By the time my mother came home, I was feeling flare-up symptoms more consistently. It was more difficult for me to eat because I was staying with the restricted diet. I tried to stay away from roughage, especially any form of fruits and vegetables, which were hard to digest. And of course, I stubbornly refused to see a doctor.

A couple of weeks passed and the symptoms became worse. I had lost much weight, and I was down to about 170 pounds by early September. I was barely eating anything except maybe a bowl of brown rice cereal once a day. It was getting difficult for me to walk because the abdominal pain kept me doubled over and I was very weak. I was struggling to climb the stairs one day when my dad stopped me.

"You know, you're dying," my father said.

"I am not," I retorted. "Shut up and leave me alone." I crawled back to my bed, which was where I had spent most of the two preceding weeks. My mother and father came into my room.

"You need a doctor," my mother said.

"They can't do anything for me," I said. "They will never find a cure for this disease."

"But you need medical attention right now!" my mother exclaimed. "This is the worst I have ever seen you look!"

"It is not. I will get better without the doctors' help. Please leave me alone," I said.

"You're breaking your mother's heart," my father said.

"Why do you have to make me the bad guy in this situation?" I asked. "This is not about you and your feelings; it is about me and my life. You have never seemed to realize that. I'm not going to the hospital just to please you. I'm tired of your bull——!"

"Let's go, Barb. Leave him alone if that is what he wants," my father said. "Sooner or later, we have to let him live his life for himself!"

"Good, leave me the hell alone," I snapped back.

Being left alone was a big deal to me. When I was suffering, I didn't want anyone to be around. I got mad when I was in pain. I was embarrassed by my condition, and I was taking it out on anyone near. I would feel the urge to hit people who were around. I have talked to some other people who have suffered from chronic illnesses, and some of them share those same instincts. I know now it is not uncommon, although no one really talks about it. At the time, it felt really abnormal.

My mother would not leave my side. She was a trooper. She was going to sit in my room until I agreed to see a doctor. So I got up from my bed and went to the couch. She followed. What a sight we must have been, me doubled over in pain and shuffling along in diapers, and her hobbling behind me on her artificial knees. I finally told her that I would call a doctor if I did not feel better in a couple days.

I was worried that I would never recover if I went into the hospital again. I told my parents that being admitted to the hospital again would break my spirit. It was something that I was proud of, the fact that I had not had a hospital stay in a long time. To me, being admitted would be like admitting defeat. I was stupid, yes, but when I talk to other people who suffer from chronic diseases or any form of pain, I realize that I am also a fierce competitor. I have an inbred strong will and a fighting spirit. The disease, however, was holding a large lead and moving on to victory.

After about three more days of no improvement, I was down to about 165 pounds, which was 50 or so fewer than I should have weighed. I woke up one morning and my tongue was so dry that it was stuck to the roof of my mouth. I went to the kitchen and drank a huge glass of water. I went back to bed but awoke about 45 minutes later, even more thirsty than the last time. I drank about 24 ounces of water, but I felt thirsty even after I finished. I knew I was in trouble. I picked up the phone and called Presbyterian University Hospital in Pittsburgh and asked to speak to Dr. Graham's secretary.

I spoke to one of her nurses, who informed me that they would have to give me a physical exam before determining whether or not I needed to be admitted. I knew I needed to be admitted, and I needed intravenous feeding badly. The new wave of health care reform made it harder for people like me to get necessary medical attention without proving how sick one is.

I asked my dad to drive me to Pittsburgh, but he was busy early in the morning so we waited until the early afternoon. It was vital to know that I could count on my parents to carry me through the tough times, no matter how strained our relationship had become during my suffering, and my making them suffer.

Dr. Graham examined me for a short period of time, and it was obvious that I had to be admitted. I needed intravenous feeding quickly to help keep the complications of dehydration from setting in. The nurses helped me onto the mobile stretcher to take me to a room in another wing in the hospital. I felt better knowing that I would be receiving hands-on medical care and much more nutrition than brown rice cereal could provide.

I figured I would be in the hospital for a week or so. I would of course have to start the steroids again but I knew I had no choice. This flare-up had progressed too far and was too vicious for me to handle on my own. I had been through this before. It was an all-too-familiar-role that I was regrettably reliving.

When the flare-ups were this vicious, it usually took one to two weeks of major steroid therapy (100 mg intravenously for a few days then 60 mg orally) before I started to recover and get back on my feet. I would always have pain in these times, but at least my appetite would come back when I took the steroids and things would start rolling in the right direction. The last phase of the flare-ups usually involved the abscesses. Some doctors said they were caused by the steroids, and others said it was just the final phase of the flare-up in the way the disease manifested in my digestive tract. I thought I would have to go through this again but be back on my feet and out of the hospital in a week, and I could nurse the abscesses in the bathtub at home until they healed.

I slept soundly the first night, but as it usually happens in a hospital, an aide woke me up for a blood sample early in the morning. I had just fallen back asleep when a team of doctors walked into the room.

"Mr. Florak?' one of them asked.

"Yes," I replied, not even half awake.

"I am Dr. Schoen," said the shortest one. He introduced the rest of his staff.

"We will be taking care of you," Dr. Schoen said. He asked the standard questions about pain, number of bowel movements, blood, appetite, and energy level. I had become so accustomed to the interrogations that I could spit out the answers before the doctors could finish the questions.

Then Dr. Schoen said the word I most feared: colectomy. It was once again all I heard. I wasn't paying too much attention to him until then.

"Let's get one thing straight, right now," I said. "That is not happening with me!"

"Look, after examining your case you would be a perfect candidate. There is no evidence of small bowel disease," he said.

"I have stated this unequivocally to everyone who has ever been involved with my case," I roared with false bravado. "I will die before I have a colectomy."

"Don't you want your life back?" Dr. Schoen asked. "Right now, you are a prisoner to the bathroom."

140

"You don't know me or what my life is like right now," I snapped. "You're not going to make that decision for me."

I could see the anger mounting in his eyes. "That is correct," he replied. "It is your decision. There may come a day, however, that you will not have a choice."

"That is fine!" I yelled. "Then my choice will be death!"

"I'm sorry that you are so against this," Dr. Schoen said. "We still need to do some tests do determine whether or not you have an abscess. We will talk to you later today."

"You can do all the tests that you want, but you will never get my colon," I replied, like a spoiled little kid trying to get the last word in, instead of a 29-year-old man.

He was right, but I couldn't bring myself to admit it. He was just another doctor to add to the list of ones that I had had the same conversation with. I had not met him before that moment, and I resented the fact that he was trying to persuade me without knowing a thing about me. The more people told me that I should have the surgery, the more I became determined to avoid it. My resolve to die in an event of the surgery became stronger.

# Chapter Fifteen

# The First Guardian

# CHAPTER FIFTEEN — THE FIRST GUARDIAN

The first test was scheduled to take place the following morning, the dreaded barium enema. I drank the radioactive liquid, which made me nauseated. When the dye started to progress through my digestive tract, I was put on the x-ray table. The x-rays have to be taken from different angles, so the patient must roll around on the table. Every time I rolled over I had to go to the bathroom. I had very little control over my bowel, and the barium would just pour out of me. It left a mess all over the x-ray room, the table, the nurses and me. I was really upset that I had to go through all the tests again. I told the doctors that I thought it would do more harm than good at this point. I mean, we were pretty sure that this was a flare-up of Crohn's disease, right?

I know that my chronic stubbornness toward medical treatment throughout the illness was a self-perceived threat to my ego and stupidity on my part. But I will always be convinced that there was no need for these tests to be done at that point. It caused me a great deal of discomfort to tell me for the one-millionth time in eight years that I had a bad case of IBD.

The doctors found no abscesses, but they felt they should do a follow-up with a full colonoscopy. They figured that since I was not taking in any food, it would not take too long to clear out my colon and have a good look. I became angry with the doctors when they told me this.

In retrospect, I should have refused the test, but I wasn't smart enough to do that. My parents had been visiting me faithfully every night, and I took my rage out on them. I cold-heartedly denounced many of the things they had said and done over the last few years in an endless tirade like a baby would have done.

I often look back at those episodes with much regret. One of the principles in Wayne Dyer's book, *Real Magic,* is to stop blaming our parents for everything and realize that they did the best that they could. They always made sure that I had the best care possible, and they gave me everything I needed. They also tried to provide emotional and psychological support that I shunned with my foolish pride. They were always there and doing better than their best. They looked past my anger and were smart enough to realize that I was not really angry with them.

All of the disappointments, in combination with the prednisone, left me in a neurotic state of mind. I would not have been a normal human being if I had not felt that way. Deep down inside, a small part of me wanted so much to live, but another part of me wanted to die. It is a tough thing for those being around a sick person to understand. I will always wonder how many people will never forgive me for shutting them out while they were trying to help me. It is hard to think about anything but yourself when you are stunned by the desperation brought on by a disease. As Simon and Garfunkel sang, "Fools say 'Ah, you do not know, silence like a cancer grows.'" It was as though I was on my own little island at the time. I could not think about anything but having to go through that colonoscopy again.

I prepped for the scope by drinking another mixture that made me vomit. I told the nurses that I could not hold any of the Go-lytely down, and they almost cancelled the test. They feared that I would not be cleared out enough to have the test done. I knew that was the last time that I could ever drink the Go-lytely. I was right.

The doctors went ahead with the test. They gave me enough anesthesia to knock me out for the entire exam. I did not know where I was for an instant when I woke up back in my room. As soon as I got my bearings, I sprinted to the bathroom.

When I got off the toilet, I became frightened. There was blood all over the place. The tender state of my colon was exacerbated by the test to the point where bleeding was induced. This had never happened before from a colon scope.

The doctors told me that I was in a terrible situation because the disease was so active. They also said that they did not find an abscess. That was all I needed to hear. It gave me false hope. The doctors shook their heads in amazement at my refusal to have the colectomy. They shrugged and told me that I could eat again in two days.

The blood in the stool continued for the first half of he next day. By the time that day ended, I was feeling that I was ready to eat. The doctors were warning me that my insurance would not cover too much more hospital time. I knew that I needed some more time of intravenous feeding before I started to eat again. My colon wouldn't be receptive to food that fast.

Nevertheless, I started to eat in two days as per doctor's orders. I tried to eat as healthfully as possible. I ate some cereal with rice milk, a piece of grilled chicken, and a sweet potato. I was encouraged because I did not experience any abdominal discomfort and I didn't go to the bathroom too much. My encouragement would be short-lived.

The doctors made arrangements to have me discharged the next morning. I could barely walk, and I was beginning to experience some rectal discomfort. It seemed always to manifest itself at the end of a flare-up. Good, I thought. I'll be on the road to recovery soon.

My thoughts turned toward what baseball practice might be like when January rolled around because I figured I would be back to normal in early November. I would have a few weeks to enjoy the holidays and get stronger before we started. It would all begin with my discharge the next day.

I rolled onto the bed and went through my pre-sleep ritual: taking many deep breaths, praying to God for healing, elevating the lower half of my body and pouring enemas into my rectum, followed by a shot-glass full of aloe vera juice to coat and soothe the skin around my backside. I would repeat the word "heal" as many times as it took for me to fall asleep.

When Dr. Schoen visited me the next morning, I had news for him. I wasn't leaving the hospital. Overnight, my testicles had swelled to the size of baseballs. I was scared to death. I knew it had something to do with the flare-up. It was bad enough that I was facing surgery that would alter how I went to the bathroom, and now I had to worry about my genitals.

What had happened was that some deep ruptures in my rectum had allowed some fluid and matter to pass through into my scrotum. The doctors were alarmed and I was stunned. A surgeon was quickly brought in along with a team of urologists. My mind was racing so quickly that I barely heard that they would attempt to make some incisions in my scrotal wall to promote drainage. The devastation of the disease was at its fiercest point.

I couldn't eat, sleep or think. There was too much adrenaline rushing through me. I was fumbling for answers or anything that would give me some hope that I would somehow pull out of the situation. The word "surreal" seems to be an overused cliché nowadays, but I almost felt like I was a third party watching this happen to someone else. I hoped this was just a nightmare from which I would soon awake.

I thought about buying the gun as soon as I went home. There were times when I was going crazy. I didn't think I was going crazy. I *was* crazy. I was still trying to fight, just out of the basic human survival instinct the rest of the time. I felt as though I were alone, watching myself star in a nonfiction horror flick.

It was at this time that God sent the first of three guardians into my life. Earlier, Dr. Gallagher had given me the phone number of one of his patients who had made a remarkable turnaround with her Crohn's disease. I called her around lunchtime that day.

When I talked to Dianne Burkhart on the phone, her voice was so comforting that it made me relax physically. She was so full of genuine concern and positive energy that she seemed like a lifelong friend. She gave me some suggestions for my diet and treatment and boosted my spirits. She also said she would pray for me and ask God to watch over me as she had asked for herself during her greatest trials with her Crohn's.

The conversation reminded me of the famous poem, "Footprints." It is the story of a man's dream in which he views scenes from his life on a beach while in the presence of the Lord. There are two sets of footprints in the sand next to each scene. During the times of the man's life in which he was most troubled, there is only one set of footprints next to those scenes. The man wants to know why the Lord left him during his greatest hour of need. The Lord then claims the footprints as His own and tells the man He will never leave him and that He carried the man through the toughest times. Someone had to have been carrying me because I was too scared to keep going.

If faced with a tough situation before I became ill, I would either run or simply snap. If I snapped, I would try to use brute force to overcome the situation. This time, a part of me had become peaceful for at least a while. Anytime you methodically plot your own death, there obviously is no complete sense of peace. I would rise and fall between serenity and calamity.

Later that night, the surgeons performed some tiny incisions in my groin and beneath my rectum. They put me under anesthesia for what they termed would be minor surgery.

The head surgeon was Dr. Ken Lee. I would have guessed him to be in his mid-to-late 30's. He had a calm, reassuring presence. He was very thorough, concerned, competent, and from his explanations, he was obviously intelligent, but he did not talk down to me. I appreciated that. I trusted him. Only once did he ask if I would consider a total colectomy, and once again I told him I would rather die than have the surgery.

The surgery took place at 9 p.m. Dr. Lee made some incisions into my groin to alleviate the swelling and give the abcesses which had formed some space in which to drain. When I awoke at 11:30 p.m., my parents were there to comfort me. I was still groggy and worn out. I had not eaten the entire day as per doctors' orders.

I could feel that there were bandages and gauze tucked deep into my left groin. At the time it didn't hurt too much, but I wasn't feeling much more than fatigue and some of the anesthesia. My mother and father left, and the surgeons came in to take a quick look at their work. I fell asleep right after they left.

The next morning, a doctor named Lisa came in. She wasn't wearing the typical white overcoat. She was friendly and very beautiful. She began asking me routine questions, and I answered them politely because she was so nice. Then she told me that the gauze would have to be changed so sterile gauze could be placed in the wound.

I propped a pillow under my backside so she could get a better look at my groin. While she was examining the wounded area, I started to think that it was the first time in a long time that I was that close to a gorgeous woman and not thinking of how attracted I was to her. Strangely, I was not embarrassed for myself to be seen like this by her, but I knew she had to feel a little awkward.

When Lisa began to pull the gauze packing from my groin, I felt the most intense pain I had ever felt in my life. I howled at the top of my lungs as though I were a werewolf barking at a full moon. For all the pain I had endured in the eight years of battling the disease, this was easily the worst. I think Lisa and the nurse were alarmed at the degree of pain that I was experiencing.

"We have a long way to go, Michael," Lisa said. "Try to relax. Take some deep breaths."

The incision Dr. Lee had made was about half an inch deep into my groin. There was a lot of gauze that needed to be pulled out. She tried to be gentle, but with a wound like that, there is no way that it would not be painful. The gauze was pinned tightly around the wound and stacked nearly a full inch thick into the half-inch space. It covered all two-and-one half inches of the wound's length.

148

During some of my other hospital stays I would hear other people's bloodcurdling screams of pain. I wondered how they could not keep their dignity. No pain in a human body could be so fierce that one would need to scream at the top of his or her lungs, could it? Couldn't those people be tougher than that? I mean, with all the abdominal and rectal pain I had experienced, sometimes I would growl and heave and breathe hard and complain and moan, but I never flat-out screamed. I would never succumb to pain that to that degree.

Lesson again in humility: I wasn't that tough. My screams were just as loud as those I heard from other people. My instance was even worse because I had a beautiful woman standing over me taking gauze out of my diseased groin area. That is what pain is all about. It took until then to understand why half the floor in a hospital wing had to hear my cries. I could hear people in the hallway outside my room saying, "What is happening to that poor man?" It is just as hard to replay in my mind other people's screams as it is to relive my own now.

When Lisa finally finished after about 30 minutes of torture, my throat hurt nearly as badly as my groin from screaming so much. Lisa immediately ordered painkillers through a morphine drip in the i.v. that was still in my arm.

The doctors told me that they would monitor my progress and that the wound would need to be cleaned several times per day. They also said that I should have the colectomy performed and warned me that if the swelling did not go down, infection could spread, and my genitals might have to be removed. I had a decision to make but I was too scared to think. I just prayed that the swelling would go down and that the fluid would leak out through the incisions.

I had been in the hospital for about ten consecutive days. I was surrounded by everything I thought could help me. There were medicine and vitamin vials all over the room. There was a bottle of holy water in the drawer next to the bed. There were heating pads and hot water bottles on the bed. There were bottles of enemas and suppositories on the bed. There was a tub of ice and cold bottles of aloe vera juice packed inside on the floor. If I were going to lose, it would not be without a fight.

I was not to eat for three days and if the swelling went down, the doctors would release me from the hospital. I was trying anything to make the swelling go down. I gave myself enemas and suppositories twice each day. I sat on the heating pad and poured aloe in to my rectum while resting in the bed with the bottom part of the mattress elevated.

My mother and father also gave me an article from a medical journal about the use of hyperbaric oxygen for the treatment of IBD. I talked Dr. Schoen into prescribing it for me, after much protest on his part.

"Those people upstairs are going to physically throw you out of this hospital," Dr. Schoen said, in reference to the administrators. "I simply am not going to be able to justify keeping you here any longer than three days."

I knew that was not nearly enough. I needed i.v. feeding without eating so that my digestive tract could heal for a week or two. Either way, I was going to try like hell.

I begged God for another chance, yet I also continued to plot my own death in case the big surgery had to be performed. The two factions of my thought processes and the morphine had my head spinning like a psychedelic rock-and-roll video from the 60's, except there was no appearance by Vanilla Fudge or Grace Slick. It was just my mind and me waging war with each other and the drugs on the inside. Milton wrote, "The mind is its own place, and in itself can make a hell of heaven or a heaven of hell." I don't know what he wrote about making a worse hell out of hell.

I was exhausted but afraid to sleep. I drifted in and out of a haze-like state. All the while, I would administer the enemas, suppositories, heating pad, holy water, and any other natural, unnatural, or superhuman entity I could think of inside my rear end.

A few phone calls from Dianne and visits from my parents would temporarily boost my spirits. In between all of this, I began treatment in the hyperbaric oxygen chamber.

The chamber is a big tube on a table with sterile blankets inside. It was barely long enough to enclose my body. I watched the Baltimore Orioles against the Cleveland Indians in the American League baseball playoffs on the television in the room. There were speakers inside the chamber and as soon as the chamber was closed, a reverse vacuum-like sensation swept through every orifice in my body. I sat in the chamber for 90 minutes at a time and continued the regimen for the next two days.

On the third day after the chamber treatments began, I spoke with Dr. Graham. She said that she wanted me to meet someone who might give me a better perspective on my situation. There was a lab technician on the staff at the hospital who had overcome his own health problems. Sometimes he spoke to patients about problems and helped them a great deal. He showed them that a positive attitude could help overcome serious illness and to lead a normal, active lifestyle. I was also told he was a martial arts teacher, which fascinated me. I greatly looked forward to meeting him.

That third day began like all the others. I had blood taken about 6 a.m., followed by a visit from a team of doctors. They asked to see if the swelling had returned, and I was happy to report that it had not. The doctors said that I could begin eating again, and they would release me the next day.

I ate scrambled eggs and some of the rice bread that my parents had bought. I also ate some fruit and had some water. I wanted to take it slowly so I wouldn't aggravate anything and bring back the swelling. I knew that this was the most fragile test that had been set before me, and every activity would have to be monitored closely. The thought of anything happening to my genitals was scary, but I still had to maintain my focus on doing all the things I needed to do every day to treat myself.

Dr. Graham called after I finished breakfast, and I told her I would have to check my schedule to be able to meet the man she wanted me to talk to. After breakfast, the packing in the wound in my groin would have to be changed. Then I would sit in the sitz bath for 30 minutes. Next would come a shower, followed by a treatment in the chamber; then lunch, which would end with a long stay in the bathroom, and then the enema/suppository/aloe/meditation treatment. I would then try to nap at 2 p.m. or so.

Around lunchtime I met the second of the three guardians God would send to help carry me through this ordeal. Elaine Hagerty was finishing her master's degree and doing some teaching in the nursing field at the university. She had just been moved to the wing of the hospital in which I was staying. She also happened to live up the street from my parents in Steubenville. Her brother Sean and my brother Mark were good friends.

Elaine was a great nurse. She took a special interest in me and told me that she would be helping me. She had much experience with Crohn's patients, and she made me feel better by just being there and being understanding.

Elaine told me that there were many people who lived productive, happy lives with ostomies. I was still very skeptical but I finally agreed to meet with the enterostomal nurse later that day. After Elaine's talk, I felt I owed it to her, my parents, and the doctors.

The nurse came in and we talked for a while. I made it clear to her that having the surgery was only in the case of an emergency. Deep inside, I was still thinking I would die before wearing the equipment that she showed me. The nurse was polite and patient, so the least I could do was afford her the same courtesy.

After about an hour, the nurse left and I reflected on some of the things she said. I wish I could say that I was more open-minded after the talk, but it didn't change a thing. I was still dead-set against the surgery. I wasn't thinking about my genitals.

I ate dinner and prepared to take a nap before I wanted to wake up at 8 p.m. The Steelers were playing the Chiefs on *Monday Night Football,* and I would be glued to the screen. The dinner went down well. I maneuvered myself to the bathroom with the help of one of the nurses and made arrangements to have a bathtub prepared for me in another wing on that floor at eight, one hour before the game's kickoff. I fell asleep about six o'clock, thinking about leaving the hospital the next day.

I didn't feel any different when I woke up. I rang the nurse who taped my i.v. lines to the pole so they wouldn't get wet. She would also wheel me down to the wing on the floor where the tub was. When she came in and I removed the bed sheet from on top of me, I gasped in horror. The swelling in the scrotal area had returned and there was stool all over the bed.

My rectum must have had several punctures in it that were permitting the stool to escape. It was also leaking through the incisions on the side of my groin that Dr. Lee had made several nights before. It was a disgusting mess. I was freaking out on the inside, but I tried to remain cool in front of the nurses. I didn't let on that anything was happening.

The only thought that went through my mind was to get to that bathtub as soon as possible. Two nurses helped me to the wheelchair. One was really good-looking and very friendly. Her name was Jill. She practically carried me onto the chair while the other one put tape on the i.v.'s and a drainage pad on the wheelchair.

I thought the bathtub would immediately drain the stool and fluid from the area. I made the water as hot as I could without burning myself.

Somehow I climbed into the tub through the wires, around the towels that Jill had set out, and past the mobile i.v. unit. I was so desperate that nothing was going to stop me from getting in that tub.

I started to beg God for help. Thoughts even crossed my mind about promising God that I would enter the priesthood if the swelling went down. I knew that if the swelling did not go down by the time I left the bathtub, I would have to choose between my colon and my genitals soon.

"Please, God, please, please, please," I begged. "Please let this pass before me. I will accept anything you have planned for me, but I really don't want to have that surgery!" Tears were streaming down my face and stool began to flood the bathtub.

"Please, God," I continued to beg. "I believe in your power. I know you can make this pass. I know it would take a miracle, but I believe in miracles. I believe in miracles." I repeated this phrase over and over again.

"Please God," I continued to reason. "Let this fate pass before me. If there is any way that I will not have to go through this, let my colon be spared. I just want to be normal." I remembered the words that Jesus had prayed to God on the night he was betrayed. I did not think I was Jesus, but I was drawing strength from the story to ask God for help.

I continued to repeat these prayers and closed my eyes and tried to will the swelling away. When I opened them the amount of stool in the tub increased each time. I became angry.

"I can't have this operation, God!" I shouted. "What about baseball? What about what others might think? What about sex? What about golf? What about other activities? Why God, why? If the surgery is meant to be, please make the decision easy on me."

After a couple of times of closing my eyes and opening them to see the situation getting worse, I suddenly remembered the words a priest once said to me: "When you are faced with what seems to be an insurmountable situation, pray for peace of mind."

It made sense. I thought about what I was doing in a dirty bathtub with scars and stitches and wires and tubes and bandages, sweating, tired, sick, and depressed. I needed something different because what I was doing wasn't working. I closed my eyes and began to pray for peace of mind. I kept asking for the decision to be made easy for me.

After a few minutes, I opened my eyes again. I looked at the mess around me and I heaved a few big sighs. I began to feel relaxed. I began to feel peaceful. I felt like a huge weight had been lifted from me. I knew what had to be done. I was not going to get any better without having my colon removed.

It was time to have the surgery.

It would be so hard. I had fought a long, brave, stubborn fight. At least I would save my reproductive organs. I found peace of mind at my worst time of crisis. The emergency situation Dr. Graham and I talked about was here, and I had an amazing peaceful perspective on it.

I rolled out of the tub. Jill would not be back to pick me up for another 45 minutes or so. I had to wheel myself down a long corridor with the i.v. in my arm, the morphine drip, and all the towels, blankets, and bandages in tow. The strain on my face did not match the sudden peace I had inside.

As I maneuvered down the corridor, the air felt so good that I felt like I was driving that wheelchair 100 miles per hour down a wide-open, tree-lined freeway on a sunny day. I turned the corner, and I could see a group of people standing near the nurses' station about 80 yards away. I couldn't make out who they were because my vision was blurred from the side effects of the steroids and the hyperbaric chamber. I heard one of them say, "What the hell is he doing?" as two of the nurses walked toward me.

"What happened?" Jill asked as she approached.

"I just realized I am wasting my time. I'm going to have to have my colon removed," I responded.

"Oh, uh, wow. When did you come to that realization?" Jill asked.

"Just now. I just realized that I can't go on like this," I said.

"How do you feel about that?" Jill asked.

"I know now that I don't have a choice," I said. "It is the right thing to do. God has made the decision easy on me."

"Is there anything I can do? Anyone I can call? Do you want to talk about this to me?" She was as nice and sympathetic as she was good-looking.

"I'm going to call my parents and tell them. Thanks for your help," I said.

Jill went on to tell me that she had treated a number of ostomy patients, and she was very encouraging. It was comforting to have the first person that I told be so positive with me. She said most people she had witnessed were able to get back to the same lives they had before they were sick. She said she could never tell the patients who had ostomies from the ones who didn't until she was told. This initial conversation meant so much to me.

I called my father. I wasn't expecting it to be a difficult conversation, but an immense amount of emotion poured out of me as soon as my father said "Hello."

"Dad, you won't have to pick me up tomorrow," I said. "The swelling came back, and I have to…." I could barely breathe between gasps and the tears that were streaming down my face. "I have to have my colon removed."

I don't remember what my dad said. I know I apologized for being such a difficult jerk. We talked for two hours, and most of it was about how scared I was. My dad reassured me that it would be the best thing for me and that I could get on with my life.

After the conversation with my father, I cried some more in the bed. It really was not because I was sad. I asked God to make the decision easy for me, and it was easy. There is no choice for a man to make between his genitals and his colon. The tears were not because I was confused, angry, or frustrated. They were more like tears of relief. It had been a volcano that had been waiting to erupt for a long time. The buildup was freeing itself from my mind, body, and spirit.

I had learned many lessons from sports, some from being involved as a competitor, some from being a fan. I knew my tears didn't mean that I wasn't tough. They were just a sign of relief, like the tears I had seen Michael Jordan and Mario Lemieux cry after winning their first professional championships in their respective sports.

Jordan and Lemieux will be remembered as champions who were arguably the best to ever play their respective sports. Neither started that way. They each took about seven years to win the championships they so much coveted. They both struggled for long periods to shake the ignominious moniker of "not being able to win the big one."

When Jordan and Lemieux both finally won their championships, the emotional relief was incredible. Sports fans can remember images of Jordan hugging the NBA championship trophy in the locker room after the Bulls won the first championship. Lemieux re-enacted that scene after the Penguins' first Stanley Cup championship.

Both men sat slumped on benches, crying their eyes out while people around them sang and danced and doused each other with champagne. The tears were every bit as much of relief from years of pressure building up and finally releasing as they were tears of joy.

That is exactly how I felt. The years of pressure and the draining struggle that had left me emotionally dehydrated finally released while I was on the phone with my father. By the time we ended the conversation, I was physically tired of even breathing. It was the most exhaustion and relief I had ever felt in my life. God had indeed made the decision easy on me and had blessed me with peace of mind.

Life was teaching me a lesson that I think I will always be trying to master. Situations that seem unbearable cause us to look to God for strength that carries us through what later seem to be minor incidents. After 29 years, I was finally coming to terms with my emotional and spiritual being, and my psychological suffering was ending. My physical pain was coming to an end, but there was more emotional pain that I had to endure.

When the surgeons came in the next day, I informed them that I would need to have the colectomy performed. They were excited as surgeons want to be when someone tells them that they want to be cut. However, they were not happy to see that the swelling in my groin area had returned. They would need to make another incision to relieve the pressure before the colectomy could be performed.

That night, another incision was made in my groin. It was almost as uncomfortable as the first. The surgeons were again concerned that infection would spread to my testicles if it did not stop. They were confident that if I had the colectomy performed, I would not encounter the swelling again. But here was a possibility that infection had already occurred in one or both of my testicles, and ultrasound tests would have to be done after the colectomy was completed to confirm or clear infection. The surgeons scheduled the colectomy in two days.

I was using the morphine drip every two hours. I used to pride myself on not even taking aspirin for pain before, but not only did the morphine help me with the worst pain I had ever felt, it also helped me sleep. I still needed to ask Dr. Lee the many questions that I had on my mind about the dramatic change that was about to take place in my life.

I managed to make a list of questions that made some sense even though my mind was clouded by the painkillers. Part of me wondered if I was able to make a rational decision while under the influence of such powerful, mind-altering drugs. My parents reassured me that I had suffered long enough and that I was doing the right thing. The surgery would lead me to a better fate.

I had one more very important person to help push me over the edge. He came to my room to reassure me and give me a great pep talk. The talk we had made me realize that having an ostomy did not define me. It was just a new part of me. It was a part of me that would make me better. This third guardian who would give me the pep talk would also make me better, and Dr. Graham was finally able to arrange for me to meet this man.

Merril Hudson has never appeared to me to be a "normal" person. He dresses impeccably finer than anyone I know. He is in tremendous physical condition, a sight easily seen even in dress clothes. He looks much younger than he is, and his presence and positive attitude are absolutely infectious.

We talked about many things, including the setbacks and odds that he had overcome. We talked about how my life was going to change and how it would all be for the better. We talked about the things that I couldn't do when I was sick that I would be able to do again in the future. Merril also said that he had studied martial arts for over 20 years and that he would give me lessons anytime I wanted. It was another amazing occurrence on this wonderfully synchronized journey God had planned for me.

I had the final push now to give me the confidence that my life would actually be better after the surgery. I asked Dr. Lee the questions I had prepared earlier. I knew better what to expect after I talked to Dr. Lee. Although I was scared, I was ready.

# Chapter Sixteen

# Two Days That Seemed Like an Eternity

# CHAPTER SIXTEEN — TWO DAYS THAT SEEMED LIKE AN ETERNITY

The surgery was two days away and I could not wait. I just wanted my life to get back to as close to normal as possible. I was looking forward to being a regular man who could function without having to wear diapers or rush to the bathroom to avoid an accident. Most of all, I looked forward to being able to eat any food that I desired and not having to worry about whether or not the food would make me sick.

The pain was the least of my concerns. I had managed it and had basically become accustomed to living with varying degrees of pain. I didn't want to become dependent on painkillers, so until the commencement of the morphine drip, I had stayed away from that type of medication. Since the surgery was only a short time away, I permitted myself very liberal use of the drip. It calmed my anxiety. I could see why it is so easy to become addicted to these drugs.

I was more relaxed around the nurses, doctors, and especially my parents. I felt better about that because we had had a few terrible fights in the previous few months. It was a hard situation for all of us, and there was so much tension that was relieved by my decision. There would be no more health crises followed by emotional crises. The doctors told me that the recovery period would be long and difficult and that my determination and attitude would be critical to my recovery. I would have to be emotionally stronger than ever..

Those two days seemed like an eternity. I was absolutely emotionally drained and relieved that the psychological war with myself was over. I had never experienced such joy, fear, sadness, optimism, relief, and determination coincidentally in such a short period in my life. I didn't reflect much at the time how much easier God had made the decision for me, but I am lucky that it happened that way because I have no regrets.

I was not very worried about my future with an ostomy. I had a strong conviction that everything would be all right. I was not concerned about the swelling in my groin, either. I had an incredible sense of peace.

I still wanted privacy about the surgery. I asked that my mother and father not tell anyone that I was even in the hospital. I needed time to be able to talk about the things that had happened. I had a great support system in addition to my friends. My parents' efforts were superhuman, and their love and support were tireless. Dianne, Elaine, and Merril showed courage and understanding that had a contagious effect on me. The nurses were especially sweet and encouraging, especially the enterstomal nurse. Dr. Lee and the rest of the doctors made me feel confident because they seemed so competent and assured. They took time to explain things to me and made me feel that I was a person and that the way I felt about things really mattered. They mapped out a timetable of expectations for my recovery period.

The hardest part was that I still had to abstain from eating. The doctors wanted my digestive system to be as empty and inactive as possible for the surgery. I went a total of eight days without eating. I knew that it would be the last time that I would ever have to go hungry in my life.

It was incredible how my life had changed in a short time. Only hours before, I was solemnly declaring the end to my life if this situation had come to fruition. Now the bewitching hour was approaching, and I was actually thinking how remarkable my future would be. I was a lucky man.

As the hours passed, the time for me to go to the operating room drew near. The surgeons came in and drew a circular mark on my side with a pen on the right side of my abdomen, about four inches to the right and one inch above my hipbone. This was where they would make the stoma. It was the part of my small intestine that would be pulled through the outside of my abdomen to empty into the ileostomy pouch.

The nurses reviewed management of the pouches, and the doctors came to talk to me again. The urologists visited me to look at my groin, and the nurses were in and out to do blood work and vital signs. It was probably a good thing that I was so occupied because it left me no time for cold feet.

The morphine added physical calm to the inner peace God had bestowed upon me. I slept much of the day when the medical people were not around. I talked with my parents briefly and they assured me that they would be there before I would be taken down to the operating room. It gave me great comfort to know that, as usual, they were by my side. I was finally beginning to appreciate their love.

On the day of the surgery, I woke up at 5 a.m. Although the surgery was scheduled to take place in the evening, I just wanted to get it over with. I dozed off and woke up again within a half hour. I had a sensation that a part of me was going to be taken away. The doctors told me that this was normal for someone facing amputation or organ removal.

I still was using the morphine at maximum dose until that morning. I was trying to save some for right before the surgery to give myself a final blast to help knock me out with the anesthesia. When my mother and father arrived in the late afternoon, I told them all I could think about was being able to eat like a normal person again. I asked them to bring some pizza for me in five days and to mark it down on the calendar. It was a type of motivation that I had used throughout the entire course of the illness because I had learned to appreciate food so much.

Merril also came by to wish me luck. It helped me to have people there to talk to, not only for support but also to take my mind off the immense challenge before me. As the time approached I began praying and asking God to make my recovery quick.

My mother and father were with me in the waiting room outside the operating room. I was surprisingly calm and relaxed. The effects of the morphine and the fatigue were really setting in. I talked with my parents for a while and tried to fight the drowsiness. I made it until about 45 minutes before the surgery was scheduled. The next time I would be conscious, I would be a changed person for the better.

I don't remember even being wheeled into the O.R. The entire operation took about three hours. I didn't feel a thing until I woke up in the recovery room. That is when the pain really came back.

I was groggy but my abdomen hurt terribly. I knew exactly what was going on around me, but I could barely communicate. I could feel that my speech was slurred, and I was rambling as I answered the nurses' questions. I told the nurse that I was in a great amount of pain, and she reminded me to hit the morphine button. When I did, I realized that the morphine supply had run out of the i.v.

I panicked. The pain was growing stronger. I hit the nurses' call button repeatedly.

"I need some painkillers right now!" I screamed. "I just had a major organ removed from my body, and I have nothing to ease the pain!"

My dad came in to check on me and I said the same thing to him. My guts had just been ripped open, and I could feel that sensation way too strongly for just coming out of surgery. I don't know if it was my fault for not telling the nurses to check the morphine supply or because the pain was greater than I expected. I raised holy hell in that recovery room and upset all the nurses there. About an hour elapsed before I received any morphine. As soon as it was administered, I fell asleep and quit complaining.

I woke up in a room that held at least five other patients. It was the worst situation that the hospital could possibly have had. It was noisy and there were people screaming in pain, including myself. The man in the bed directly across from me told the nurse that he was the recipient of a kidney transplant, and that he was sick because he had been drinking beer earlier that day. He was resting with his feet on the floor and his head in the middle of the mattress, and he soon began snoring like a wild boar in a fight with a buzz saw. There was no private bathroom, and I hadn't yet learned how to operate the ostomy pouch to relieve the waste. There was only one nurse for all of the patients in the room. It seemed as though we all needed her attention every minute.

I wondered if the surgery had been the right thing to do. I was miserable in that room. I knew that I had to get out of there. I was in pain and not getting enough attention. I was also angry and not in a good frame of mind. I exchanged unpleasantries with the nurse and I yelled at her until she left the room.

My parents had Dr. Graham arrange a private room for me. I finally left the recovery room the next day next day, exhausted as much from the lack of sleep and my anger as the operation itself. It was almost midnight when I was wheeled into the private room. The nurse said that all of my records and orders were being transported to the nurses' station on that floor. She said my physical therapy would start the next day and that I would have to start getting out of bed, which I hadn't done in three days.

I was scared that the stitches might tear open even though they were on the inside of the skin. I was also afraid of the immense pain. I was still able to use the morphine, which I did as much as possible. I also wanted to go at my own pace, and I was afraid that the doctors and nurses would try to rush me, not realizing that I wasn't the normal person just coming out of ostomy surgery. I was much weaker. I wasn't quite out of the woods.

There was still the situation with my groin to be concerned about. The swelling had subsided a little but not totally. My legs were weak because I had been bedridden for most of the last two months. The doctors stressed the fact that the more I got moving, the quicker I would totally recover. I was apprehensive because of the pain of the surgery and the other concerns. I was physically weaker than I had ever been, and it would be imperative for me to have the best care possible.

The next morning the nurse came in to take my vitals. Her name was Jan. She was a little older than me and she was short. She had short, neat hair, and red-rimmed glasses. She talked quickly and told me what I was going to do that day. The itinerary included getting out of bed for the first time since the surgery. Until then, the nurses had been emptying the pouches for me. Now I would have to learn how to walk again to get to the bathroom to empty the pouches myself.

Jan was a tough cookie. She was more than a foot shorter than me, but she dragged me out of bed. The hardest part was the beginning, trying to roll over to start the move. I had to use my abdominal muscles at least a little to start. As soon as I started to roll, I could feel where Dr. Lee had cut my abdominal wall in half. I screamed out and I had to stop.

Jan told me to put a pillow on my abdomen and put as much pressure on it as I could stand with my hand. This helped control the pain and enabled me to get going. I put both feet on the floor for the first time in almost a week, and I staggered like a newborn colt. Jan propped me up.

I took slow steps, using the i.v. pole almost like a cane, clutching the pillow in the other hand and pressing on my abdomen. I couldn't stand up straight. I probably looked like a 100-year-old man, but I didn't notice anyone staring at me. My vision was so blurred from the steriods and the hyperbaric chamber that I couldn't see ten feet in front of me. I started to heave and my legs were quivering.

I was close to falling. I thought about the stitches coming apart, about the i.v.'s ripping out, and about falling on my stoma.

"Jan…help!" I said.

"Listen, you're doing great," Jan said to me. "Expect to struggle at first, but things will be fine. I'll be here every step of the way."

The encouragement helped. It calmed my fears. Jan sounded so confident. She put her arms around me and told me to grab the railing on the wall and put the pillow in my other hand. She grabbed the i.v. pole.

"I got you," she said. "Just put one foot in front of the other."

I don't remember what happened the first time my mother had showed me how to ride a bike, but I bet it was similar to this. I had a grin of amazement on my face. I never thought walking could be so pleasurable.

I walked about 35 feet down the hall and turned around. I went slowly back to my room. It was hard to get back into bed. My legs felt like I had just done ten sets of heavy squats. I didn't exactly have the stamina of a marathon runner. Getting back to the active duties of being a baseball coach seemed like an eternity away.

I thought about whether or not I would be able to return to baseball. The doctors assured me that I would and that the recovery process would speed up. I had almost three months until practice would start, and I wanted to make sure that I at least appeared to be in normal health.

That is one of the reasons that I had asked my mother and father to keep what happened confidential. I did not want anyone to feel sorry for me. Pity doesn't get you out of bed. I didn't want to talk about it to anyone outside my own family. I would discuss it at my own pace. I didn't feel that it was a big deal, especially not as much as I first thought it might be. I was so relaxed and at peace with what had happened that I just wanted to get on with the recovery and the rest of my life.

There was more reason to be concerned with the swelling in my groin. A spot appeared on my left testicle. I called it to the attention of one of the urologists when he came to check on me that night.

The urologist identified the spot as a point where fluid and mucosal buildup were trying to release. He said that the fluid needed to be released and that making an incision would be the only thing to help. He left the room and came back with some surgical equipment. He shot my groin up with Novocaine and made a small incision. Fluid came rushing out of the hole and ran all over my legs and the bed.

"Wow, I have never seen anything like this before," the urologist said.

I had heard these words from a doctor before. It was yet another time during the course of the illness that specialists were called in to photograph a part of my body that was abnormally diseased. The doctors always asked if I minded having the photographs taken. I always permitted them to do so because it would help the study of the disease.

As the fluid continued to drain, the doctors told me something else I did not want to hear: this wound would also have to packed with sterile gauze and changed at least three times per day. Things looked like they may continue to get worse before they got better.

There were many concerns that the doctors had for me. Obviously, just having my colon removed presented a huge challenge for recovery. I had lost most of the muscle mass in my body, and I could barely stand up.

There were now two wounds in my groin that needed to be dressed and changed several times a day. Both wounds had the potential to become infected. My weight was down below 160 pounds. Although I had received two units of blood during the surgery, my blood count was still low.

Through all the bad things that kept happening, I retained an incredible sense of optimism. I could really see the light at the end of the tunnel. Even the nurses and doctors were astonished at the transition my attitude had undertaken. I couldn't take much credit for that, though. I knew that God had blessed me not only with a great supporting cast, my own strong will, and a second chance but also with a real opportunity to make something positive out of something negative.

I could not wait to get out of the hospital. The next few days were hard. I learned how to operate the ostomy pouch (Coloplast products were the best fit for me), how to change the packing in the wounds myself, and how to eat and walk again. I had a long road ahead but I permitted myself to focus only on positive things. I also knew there was one thing that I would be able to do that many people would envy: eat whatever kind of food I wanted and however much I wanted.

The doctors were going to permit me to start eating and release me if everything went smoothly. I had my mother and father sneak a couple pieces of pizza in the day before I was allowed to start eating. It was cold and soggy, but it was the best meal I ever had in my life. The appreciation for food will stay with me the rest of my life. I rarely skip meals and most of the meals I eat now are hearty.

Those things kept me motivated. The doctors told me there was one more hurdle that I hadn't cleared. I needed an ultrasound test on my testicles to see if there was any infection.

I was not worried at all, though. I had been going to the rehab center in the hospital to get hot baths to stimulate draining. The swelling had been reduced, and despite the physical evidence that was scary, I just had an inner knowing that everything would be all right. After the tests were performed and the nurses came back with good results, my beliefs were correct. My testicles were healthy and I was on my way.

When my father wheeled me out of the hospital, I was not sad at all about the changes that my body had undergone. I had no time to dwell on my negative past. I was strictly determined to get on with my life.

# Chapter Seventeen

# Gaining Courage, Strength, and Confidence

# CHAPTER SEVENTEEN — GAINING COURAGE, STRENGTH, AND CONFIDENCE

The first two weeks at my parents' home, I had nurses come to help me change the packing in the wounds and teach me how to change and work with the ostomy appliances. After that time period, I was on my own because the insurance company would pay for only so much. My parents offered to help with the dressings and the appliance but these things were a bit too personal not to have professionals to do the work.

After a couple weeks, I was still not moving around too well. I had three more weeks until Thanksgiving, and the doctors said I could begin exercising then. I tried to stay on my feet as much as possible without being too strenuous. I was fatigued from the whole ordeal and still taking painkillers. I would need every bit of those three weeks to get my necessary energy level back.

The wounds started to heal quicker than expected. The doctors thought that my immune system might be impaired from the prolonged steroid use, causing the wounds to heal slower than they normally would, but I was lucky. I had to dress the wounds only a few times before they closed on their own. About the same time, my energy level began to rise and my legs and abdominal wall began to strengthen.

This Thanksgiving would be a special one. I was getting about my eighth "second chance" and this time I knew I would take advantage of it. The doctors were finally giving me some good news. After a series of follow-up visits, the urologists said that the recovery was going well. The swelling had disappeared. I began to see a psychologist to make sure that I was not in denial about my new life.

I had always been opposed to support groups because I was such a private person. I valued the anonymity that one-on-one counseling provided. It helped very much to be able to talk about my fears and my feelings to someone who was not emotionally attached to my case.

The sessions made me feel stronger. Combined with my increased physical strength, I had a confidence that I never had before. That may have been strange for someone who was trying to gain over 60 pounds and learning how to walk and go to the bathroom again, but that was how I felt. I knew that I had a purpose. I had to be an example of how to overcome adversity and teach baseball. I would soon have the physical strength that would permit me to do my job with the effort and the passion I knew it would take to be effective.

When Christmas rolled around, I was ready to talk about coaching again. I talked to Dave Walkosky and we made plans about the team. Dave also told me to be ready because he was looking to move from Waynesburg to another college football job.

I thought about the possibility of being a head coach. It crossed my mind for a brief moment that I wasn't ready, but the things that I had just fought through gave me the self-assurance I needed. I kept repeating a quote I read from Eleanor Roosevelt:

*You gain courage, strength, and confidence by every experience in which you really stop to look fear in the face. You are able to say, "I lived through this horror. I can take the next thing that comes along." You must do the thing you think you cannot do.*

Thinking about inspirational themes like this one and addressing my fears helped me overcome any trepidation I had about being able to do anything. I wasn't thinking much about Dave's leaving. I thought he would stay. The college would just find another football/baseball coach if he did leave, I thought. I know how hard it is to find coaching jobs. I basically dismissed the thought.

I continued my recovery through the New Year. I started slowly with my physical fitness workouts. First I climbed up and down the stairs ten times a day and did some exercises with five-pound dumbbells. After a couple weeks, I was able to lift weights for one-half hour per day. I slowly built myself up to the 45-55 minutes per day to which I was accustomed.

I started to notice muscle mass returning after about six weeks of lifting. I was slowly gaining weight, and enjoying the changes in my body. The stoma was low enough on my waistline that I could go shirtless and not have anything be noticed.

The management of the ostomy was less difficult than I imagined. It only took a minute to empty, and I became better at changing the pouches when it was necessary. The ostomy did not impair my weightlifting or any activity in any way. I was careful not to bump or drag any weights across my abdomen, but having the ostomy made my workouts better because I was gaining energy and did not feel sick at all. My appetite was ferocious, and I was enjoying foods that I hadn't thought about eating in years.

I didn't wonder for a second why I had waited so long to have the surgery and get on with my life. I knew it had to involve two outstanding doctors like Gr. Graham and Dr. Lee. I understood that I had needed the unwavering support of my parents. I knew that I had to have Merril, Dianne, and Elaine walking me through the tough times. I understood that the emergency situation had to arise for me to agree to take the final step. I knew that I would have to be at the height of my suffering and humility to ever have the surgery.

I didn't understand, though, why God didn't come through with a miracle for me. What I had begged God for did not come true. My colon was not healed and was no longer even inside of me. It took me until one day in early January to gain a little understanding.

I started to go out in public again in January of 1997, and part of my routine was to go to bookstores and read or buy self-help and inspirational books. I was in the Borders Book Store in Cranberry Township, Pennsylvania, when I came across a book that helped me to a new way of believing and understanding the events in my life.

I saw a book by an author I hadn't heard of before named Marianne Williamson. The book's title was *A Return to Love*. I don't know what led me to the book, but I picked it up, read the back cover, and took it to the register to buy without thinking about it at all.

The book was an interesting philosophical work about how love can conquer all fears that human beings have. It also echoed many of the thoughts of Wayne Dyer, especially the one about trusting in God's plan and letting it take you down the path that God has chosen for you.

One part of the book discussed miracles and what people's expectations of miracles are. Williamson writes that miracles occur every day. She believes that miracles are not always a change in events or physical conditions but a change in our perception of the situation.

I started to reflect on my circumstances after I read this thought. I realized that what had happened to me was a miracle. I had begged God for a physical miracle that never happened. I did receive a miracle in the fact that my perception of the situation was changed. I didn't receive a physical healing of Crohn's disease but rather a healing of my perception of what life would be like with an ostomy. I was amazed at how profound I believed this book to be and how at peace I was with the path that my life was on. I was forced to suffer great physical pain to heal my mind and spirit. Not only was it a miracle that I survived all the physical, mental, and spiritual anguish, but it was even more of a miracle that my horrible attitude had changed. As the Biblical book of John says, *This is the confidence we have in approaching God: that if we ask anything according to his will, he hears us.* It was God's will that I overcome the disease through surgery and it happened.

It would be a shame to waste my special talents that God has given to me. Everyone has a purpose. My communication skills and my experience in baseball were my biggest assets. I looked forward to putting them into practice at Waynesburg. During sessions with the psychologist in mid-January, I decided that I had too much work to do to feel sorry for myself.

I was anxious to get back to Waynesburg. Dave and I were building a program based on all the old-fashioned values with which we were raised and trained. The kids coming back were excited about the season and they were becoming better baseball players. Dave had done a good job of recruiting some good athletes in the freshman class.

We told the kids from day one that we expected to win the Presidents' Athletic Conference title. The first meeting was full of enthusiasm and optimism. Dave and I planned the practice schedule for the first week. We were sorry to hear that our good friend, Richard Krause, would not have the time to coach with us this year.

I was a little hesitant about managing the ostomy and going through practice. I hated to miss one second to leave to go to the bathroom. There is always the fear in the back of my mind that the pouch might break or leak. Those things are minor concerns, and my peace and confidence with the situation gave me strength to overcome those concerns.

I thought about how much better this season would be. I would have the strength and the energy to coach with the intensity that made me a better coach. I wouldn't have to worry about running from the third base coach's box to the bathroom. My concentration would no longer be divided between baseball and pain.

By the second week of February, practice was in full swing. Spring trip was only a few weeks away, and things seemed to be going smoothly. Then Dave gave me some news that would change my life rapidly.

Dave badly wanted to leave Waynesburg to move back to the Division

I level. He told me that he was interviewing soon for an assistant football coaching position at the University of Tennessee-Martin and that if he were offered the job he would leave immediately. He said he would go all-out to recommend me for the head baseball coach's job that he would leave vacant at Waynesburg.

A whirlwind of thoughts went thorough my head. What if Dave left and I got the job and I wasn't ready? Or worse, what if Dave left and the college decided to hire someone from the outside? Of course, we didn't reveal these things to the kids on the team until they became reality.

During the third week of February, Dave interviewed for the job in Tennessee. We still went along with business as usual. Practice was going very well but we were concerned about how the kids might handle the change. We did not want any distractions. We knew it would be another week before Tennessee-Martin decided whether or not to hire Dave as their defensive coordinator. To be prepared for the best, Dave reviewed the administrative tasks of the baseball job with me. He also reviewed his duties as sports information director with me so that I would also be ready to handle that tier of the job. I possessed the necessary qualifications and skills for that part, too.

After a week went by, Dave finally received the call. He would leave for Tennessee the week before the Waynesburg College baseball team was to go on spring trip. The team went into a minor state of uncertainty but I stayed calm.

The school did not make a move for a week. Dave assured the team that he was pushing me for the job. I acted as head coach while Dave went through the relocation process and tied up loose ends. I didn't demand anything from the school. I just had an inner faith that everything would work out for the best. I told the players that in the event I was not named head coach, I would prepare them so the new coach would have a smooth transition. Although I believed that I was the best candidate, I knew I was not the only one.

I had all my references, including Coach Carbone, Coach Toadvine, Matt Morrison, and all the other friends that I had as baseball coaches, call the administrators for me. I placed the situation in God's hands. I was not concerned.

After some negotiations, the college finally drew up a contract for me to be the head baseball coach, sports information director, and professor of communication. It would be a challenge doing all of these duties, but I wouldn't have to worry too much about the SID part in the spring since there was no football or basketball going on during that time and I would not teach until fall semester. That left me to concentrate fully on my first head coaching job. We had three days to get ready for the trip.

Being named a college head coach was a far cry from having a major organ removed from my body just half a year earlier. I felt a sense of achievement but also a sense of great responsibility and humility. The things that I had been through assured me that I would be humble, and I owed a lot to the kids on the team who supported me when I was trying to get hired. It gave me a positive, nervous energy that I hadn't experienced since I had competed in athletics as an athlete more than seven years before.

Dave had made all the reservations for the Florida trip before we left. We had become very good friends and would stay in close contact. He would be able to help me with any questions I had. The softball team was traveling with us, and their coach had been through a few of those trips before. The on-the-field coaching would be a difficult challenge. I didn't have time to hire an assistant coach. It would be 27 players and me by ourselves.

We won our first game but after that things got rough. I was very assertive with my belief about discipline, and on the third day, a few guys were late for breakfast. We lost a couple of games that I thought we should have won because we were flat. The following morning, four players, including our top pitcher, Brian McFarland, slept in and missed breakfast. We lost a doubleheader that day.

In hindsight, we weren't that good. I had expected us to be better, and I wanted much more emotion from the kids than what we played with. I made them understand that we expected to win and that mediocrity and tardiness for team events would not be tolerated. After the doubleheader, I made the team run 60-yard sprints for a half hour in 97-degree heat. They were not happy to say the least, but no one was late for breakfast, or anything else, anymore.

During the doubleheader, I benched two of our three senior captains for mistakes they made to send a message to the team. It was hard because they had been two of the most vocal people in support of me for the job. I had to let them know that mental mistakes were unacceptable, especially from seniors. The whole team was upset with me, and no one would speak to me other than to ask for dinner money. I knew in my heart, however, that I was doing the right thing.

We survived the trip and won a few more games. We had some work to do to get the record above .500 and to be able to challenge for the Presidents' Athletic Conference title. The team began to play much better as soon as we came home. We spent much of our time on hitting because at the Division III level, not very many teams have good pitching and defense, so our strategy would be to try to be as potent offensively as possible. Hitting is the part of the game that I believe I know best. It is also the aspect of baseball that many kids believe to be the most fun. I thought one way to build enthusiasm would be to spend a lot of time practicing hitting, base running, and aggressive offensive play. The kids believed this and began to see themselves improve every day.

We continued to build momentum heading into the conference tournament, thinking that we had a good chance to win. We had a winning record in the conference and pushed our overall mark above .500. We played hard-fought games with Washington and Jefferson College who had finished just ahead of us in first place during the regular season.

We began the double-elimination championship tournament with a win, but we lost the next game to W&J. They were tough kids, and many of them also played on their nationally-ranked football team. We felt we were better prepared than they were, and we desperately wanted a rematch.

We had to get by Thiel College in the losers' bracket game, which was not easy, because we had to play one hour after the loss to W&J. The kids picked themselves up and played great in a 26-8 win. We had 25 hits in the game, and we knew we were really clicking offensively. We would need that same type of effort in two days because we had to beat W&J twice on their field. They would need to win only one game.

McFarland was questionable for that day. He had thrown 130 pitches three days earlier in our opening round, a 14-8 win over Bethany College. He came into my office at nine o'clock in the morning of the championship game with an electric stimulator on his arm.

"Coach, I'm ready to go today," Brian said.

"Are you sure?" I asked. "The last thing I want to do is get you hurt."

"Yeah, I want to pitch," he said.

The look on his face left me with no doubts. As a freshman, he was the league's best pitcher. He is a tough-as-nails kid from Martins Ferry, Ohio, and one of the fiercest competitors I have ever known. I knew we would at least have a great chance to win the first game. As we traveled a half-hour up Route 79 to Washington, Pennsylvania, I wondered if our bats would stay hot. Our guys answered that question soon after we got off the bus.

We hit three home runs in the very first inning. Every ball that was hit in the entire inning was hit hard, even the outs. W&J was shocked. Not only did we refuse to roll over and die, but we also were throwing our biggest punches from the opening bell.

I preached positively to the players about what a war the whole day would be. W&J would not quit. We were so filled with positive emotion that we felt unstoppable. The final score of the first game was 16-8, and we totaled 15 hits. We jumped out to an early lead in the second game, also. We scored seven runs in the first two innings, but I was concerned about how thin our pitching had become. Most of the kids had sore arms and we had Nate Miller, a talented but inexperienced sophomore, on the mound. He hadn't pitched more than three consecutive innings the whole year.

Nonetheless, I tried to fill the players with positive emotion. Sometimes, when a coach disciplines his players, kids mistake discipline for negativity. I knew our players were very disciplined. There was nothing left to do but blow out the positive emotion and desire to win that we had bottled up inside us. I kept encouraging the kids and telling them to dig deeper and finish the job. I stressed how much fun this experience was.

In between innings, I jogged past the W&J dugout. Every time I passed their head coach, former Pittsburgh Steeler defensive lineman Jon Banaszak, he just shook his head in disbelief. Their assistant coach, Mike Mason, said, "Every time we play you guys, it's a war."

"Win or lose, this has been fun. This is what it is all about," I replied. I had learned through my health crisis to appreciate the journey and not the end. Wayne Dyer writes of detaching oneself from the result and enjoying the path. I successfully learned to do this. Even though it was only the third inning, I was consumed with appreciation for the enthusiasm, dedication, and improvement my players were showing.

W&J came roaring back. I had to take Nate out of the game in the third inning. We started to use pitchers that were simply out of gas. By the fifth inning, W&J had taken a 12-8 lead. I didn't know what we would do. While sitting on the bench during the bottom of the fifth inning, I felt a tap on my shoulder. It was McFarland.

"Put me in," he said.

"I won't do that to you," I replied. I had no doubt in my mind that he would shut them down, but there was no way that I could ask him to pitch after he had thrown over 250 pitches in three days.

"I'm telling you, my arm is fine and I want to pitch," Brian said.

We had a short discussion. I told him that his future was more important to me than winning the championship. I tried to talk him out of it, but he would not relent. I finally decided to send him out to the mound after we could still not get anyone out.

Brian came in, and, of course, shut them down. Our bats rallied and we closed the margin to 12-11. But we just couldn't push the last run across, and we lost the championship by one run.

I was so proud of the way our kids fought that I had tears in my eyes as they tried to overcome the toughest circumstances they could possibly face. Our seniors came up big. Tom Ricco and Clint Zvolenski each had homers and drove in three runs. The display of guts on McFarland's part was absolutely incredible, and the whole team believed we could win the tournament after coming all the way out of the loser's bracket. I really appreciated the team's effort. Even though we had just lost, I was as happy as I had ever been on a baseball field.

My first season as a college head coach turned out to be a memorable one. Most of the kids improved greatly as the season progressed. Many of them communicated to me that they learned lessons about discipline, sacrifice, and hard work. They also said that they did not know that they could be that good individually or collectively when the season started but that I helped them believe it as the season continued.

How good we had become didn't really sink in until two weeks after the season had ended. I saw the NCAA news, which published the year's final season statistics for Division III baseball in a late May issue. To my surprise, our team led all Division III baseball teams in the country with a .382 team batting average! It was a great achievement, and although we didn't expect it, we were very proud and felt deserving because of all the hard work we had put in.

The batting title was the icing on the cake for a good start. The program was set to take off. I had to bring in some great recruits for us to make the jump, so I would be busy scouting western Pennsylvania and eastern Ohio for talent. Although I was beginning to feel stronger every day, the building of the program would temporarily take a back seat to another minor health crisis.

# Chapter Eighteen

# We Broke the Punch Bowl

# CHAPTER EIGHTEEN — WE BROKE THE PUNCH BOWL

In the middle of the 1997 season, I had begun to notice horrible red welts on my forearms and lower legs. They developed into open wounds that needed bandages because they were bleeding and openly draining.

I saw a dermatologist when they first began to appear, and he prescribed a treatment for what he determined was pyoderma gangrenosa, as skin condition that is sometimes associated with Crohn's. The treatment did not work and by late May, my whole right leg began to swell. I went to the emergency room at PUH, and the dermatologist was called back in.

This time an entire team of dermatologists came to see me. By consensus, they announced that it was the worst case of pyoderma gangrenosa they had ever seen. Again with my permission, pictures were taken to document an extreme instance of Crohn's disease manifesting itself somewhere on my body.

The dermatologist told me that the only thing that would reduce the swelling in my leg and clear up the sores was prednisone. I had refused to take it several weeks before when it was first prescribed. I wanted no part of prednisone because of the side effects with the bloated cheeks, mood swings, and other side effects. But the skin condition had become so advanced that my entire leg was swollen, and there was a chance that a major infection could develop. Against my wishes but out of sheer necessity, I began a medium dose of prednisone that would last a total of two months.

The mood swings returned again. I had ugly blemishes on my extremities and acne all over my face. It was the beginning of summer, and I had to try to see as many ball games as I could. The easy thing for me to do would have been to stay inside and pout, but my inner strength and newly found confidence pushed me forward.

I knew there were things that I had to do. I had to get some good players to push us over the hump to win the championship. I had to continue to lift weights myself and build my own physical strength, and I had to relearn how to play golf. Hobbies are an important outlet for stress for someone involved in a strenuous profession like coaching. I wanted to live life to the fullest and experience all the things that the disease had restricted me from fully enjoying before the surgery.

Tour de France champion and cancer survivor Lance Armstrong once said, *"If you ever get a second chance in life at something — go all the way."* I knew what my mission in life was and I couldn't let something like a few nasty blemishes on my skin hold me back now. I just put large bandages over the sores and went to work.

I had sacrificed a lot to keep that position at Waynesburg. The sports information director's job was time-consuming and challenging. I was also barely making enough money to make ends meet. I believed, however, that good things in life come only through hard work and sacrifice. I relay this message to my players every chance I get.

We needed more athletic, bigger, stronger players to beat W&J and the other teams in our conference. They overpowered us even though we were more fundamentally sound. We needed a couple of pitchers, as every baseball team does. More than anything, however, we needed some strong guys who could hit. I began scouring our recruiting area for kids to fit the bill.

At first it was slow but it picked up toward the end of the summer. I was relentless. I saw over 100 baseball games that spring and summer, sometimes seeing three or more games in a day. It paid off. We wound up having a great recruiting class, and I felt we would have an excellent opportunity to win the conference.

When school began in late August, we landed two key parts to our drive for the championship. Charlie Humes, a power-hitting shortstop who had played for Matt Morrison, and Tommy Cannon, a quality pitcher from New Philadelphia, Ohio, enrolled in school during the first week. They both came with challenges for me, but I knew that I could make a great impact on them athletically, academically, psychologically, and personally.

Our fall practice session went well. The returning players all improved and the freshmen were even better than I thought they would be. We were poised to have a great season.

I was really enjoying teaching the classes and being an academic advisor. It was rewarding, and I received much positive feedback from the administration and the students. With the SID work added on I was working over 60 hours a week even though I was technically part-time. I knew what needed to be done and that hard work and sacrifice were the only way I knew how to do things. Socializing was minimal and I could not afford many luxuries.

I lived in an apartment that had no heat in it for the entire month of November. I slept in three sweatshirts, three pair of sweatpants and socks, and a ski cap underneath four covers on the bed. The apartment was dirty, and there was a family of raccoons living in the walls for a while. I washed some of my clothes in the shower because I didn't have money to do laundry, but I knew one day all of this would be worth it.

The players and I discussed what the feeling would be like for us to carry the championship trophy off the field after the last game. We did not talk in "ifs"; we talked in "whens." I told the players not to *think that we could* win the championship, rather, to *know we were going* to win the championship.

I still kept a tight reign on the discipline. I demanded that the kids be on time, that they have no facial hair below their upper lips, wear no earrings, give 110 percent every day, and represent the team and the college in a first-class manner everywhere we went. We also had study tables four times a week.

The hard work and discipline paid off. We received compliments about the behavior of the team everywhere we went. They bought into the discipline and we were prompt, dedicated, and hard-working. Fifteen of the 31 players had grade point averages of over 3.0 in the year's first semester.

As the New Year turned we began to get ready for the year's second semester. The only thing I heard from the players was how they could not wait until the season started. I tried to be the rational voice, but I was so excited that I could barely contain myself.

The day before the semester started, I shaved all the hair off my head. Part of it was the emotion I felt when my dad and I watched the Steelers lose a heartbreaking AFC championship game to John Elway and the Denver Broncos the day before. It was mostly a symbol, however, of how excited I was and the intensity I would bring to the 1998 Waynesburg College baseball season.

I kept telling the players at each practice that I had a very good feeling about the team. I knew we had the best team in the conference. We had talent at all positions and we had some depth. We had the pitching that is is always the most important part of any baseball team. We had a "stopper," which in baseball terms means a pitcher that your opponents are afraid of, in Brian McFarland. We also knew that we could hit because we had proved it the year before.

Our spring schedule was rough. We played against a few nationally ranked teams, and our pitching wasn't ready yet. We also had some bad luck and some problems with our travel arrangements.

When we returned home from the trip, I found out that almost half the team had been drinking on the trip, which was explicitly against team policy. We were in turmoil, and I thought we might be losing a grip on what was supposed to be a championship season.

I was really disappointed in the kids for drinking because it meant to me that maybe there wasn't as much support for my beliefs as I thought there was. I was also disappointed in the way I handled the situation, although it turned out to be the thing that saved our season.

I punished the guilty parties severely. They ran punishment sprints and other exhausting drills that had nothing to do with baseball and were suspended for four games. I read the riot act to them while they ran because I wanted to send a message. A couple of them quit the team after a heated exchange of harsh words with me.

Regardless of what any coach says, it hurts to punish kids when you know they are good kids. Nonetheless, they are kids and they make mistakes. Some of the kids held it against me that I was so hard on them, but rules are rules. We lost one of our best players over the incident, and I thought we might lose some more, but I had to hold my ground. My coaches had done the same when my teammates and I were caught in similar situations, and I respected them for it.

I called a team meeting, which we held in private. At the meeting, I basically bared my soul to the team. It was not a ploy to get them back on my side but an attempt to toughen them up. I shared with them the most intimate details of my life and let them know that I was far from perfect myself. The players then knew that my life was tough but I was tougher and that I wanted them to be the same way.

I also brought up the example of the battle that my assistant coach, Mike Humiston, and his family fought every day. Mike is very proud of the fact that he is a former NFL player. He is even more proud of his son, Ben, who has muscular dystrophy and the love that his family has for one another.

I walked out of the meeting and simply told the guys that if they thought

Mike and I could teach them anything about overcoming the adversity we were facing that they should show up at practice the next day with a better attitude. It was a very emotional scene for me but one that would help bring the team much closer together and help us in the long run.

We dropped two games at Muskingum College before the suspended players returned. We then responded like I knew the team was capable of doing. We had only a couple of weeks to get ready for the tournament but we caught fire. We won ten games in a row heading into the conference tournament. We had a few new players in the lineup, but we still knew we were the best team in the league heading into the postseason.

Bethany had beaten us twice during the regular season, and they had the highest seed for the tournament. We beat W&J in the first game as McFarland pitched an outstanding game. We were confident against Grove City the next day. We had beaten them four times in four games during the regular season. We had our number two pitcher, lefthander Ben Westrick, fresh and ready to go. Grove City was even more ready. They did a good job of putting the bat on the ball, and everything they hit found a hole. They beat us for the first time that season, 11-4. We had to stay and play Bethany on their home field. The winner of that game had to beat Grove City twice at Grove City the next day.

I kept telling our guys to stay positive and that we were still going to win the whole thing. I told them that it would be more satisfying to come out of the losers' bracket to win it all. We claimed an early lead but Bethany rallied to take a 4-1 advantage. Our pitcher, Jim Peck, was pitching his guts out and held them at bay.

In the fourth inning, our kids showed how much guts they had. Freshman Jason Lowman homered to bring us back within two runs. Two hits and an out later, catcher Bob Showman came to the plate.

I gave Showman the bunt sign. It was an unorthodox move, considering there was one out with runners on first and third and the fact that Showman did not run well. He was a great bunter, though, and put down a perfect bunt that caught Bethany off guard. Their third baseman threw the ball into right field and we tied the game.

Lowman hit another home run the next inning. Cannon pitched the last inning and one-third to shut the door. We were on our way to a rematch with Grove City for the title. Just like the year before, we would have to win twice on our opponent's home field, and they would have to win only once.

Coach Bahen had a saying for big games when we were playing on an opponent's home field. He would say that we were going to crash their party, drink the punch, and break the punch bowl. I used that for our battle cry when I talked to the kids about winning twice at Grove City.

We had a great challenge in front of us. We were playing our fourth and fifth (if we won the fourth) games in four days. Our kids were tired, and we were scheduled to leave from Waynesburg's campus at 8 a.m. to make the two-hour bus ride to Grove City. I wondered how our kids would respond. We scheduled batting practice in our gym at 7 a.m.

When I walked into the gym at 6:45 a.m. the next morning, I knew we would win the championship. More than half of the team was already there taking batting practice early. I was more proud of the fact that the kids were that dedicated than anything else we did that year.

We arrived at Grove City early. As the bus sat in the parking lot, I told the kids to close their eyes and envision the things we were going to do: pitchers hitting their spots; hitters getting their pitch and hitting the ball hard; fielders making smooth catches and strong, accurate throws. Most of all, I told the kids to envision us carrying the championship trophy off the field at the end of the day.

The first game was easy for us. McFarland pitched another outstanding game. Adam Jack, a Grove City native and our senior captain, hit a three-run home run, and we won easily, 9-1. We knew the second game would be much tougher.

Chris O'Connor was a sophomore spot starter for us, and I thought he was a year away from being a good pitcher that we could rely on to be a force in our rotation. He was the only pitcher we had with a fresh arm. He was a competitor and a very intelligent kid.

Chris came up huge for us. Grove City had a couple big hitters that we knew would kill us if we weren't careful. Chris got them out and kept us in the game. We took an early lead but Grove City fought back.

We were winning by one run in the bottom of the sixth when Charlie Humes came through with a big two-run single to push our lead to 4-1. I brought Cannon in to pitch the last inning and close out the championship for us. Our players who were not in the game were on the edge of the field, poised to rush the pitcher's mound to celebrate the championship after we recorded three outs. Grove City would not die, though. They got a few seeing-eye hits and rallied back to tie the game 4-4. We couldn't score a run in the bottom of the seventh, so the championship had to be decided in extra innings.

I could feel the wind come out of our sails a little. Our kids had fought so hard and had taken an early lead and deserved to win. Grove City spoiled our celebration. I just told the kids to keep pushing and that we would win. I told them to know that. I just felt it was our destiny.

Neither team had any good scoring opportunities in the eighth or ninth innings. There were a couple great defensive plays on both sides. As I jogged by Grove City's bench in between innings, I told their coaches, Rob Skaricich and R.J. Bowers, that it didn't get any better than what we were seeing. It was déjà vu from the great championship against W&J the year before.

We loaded the bases with no one out in the bottom of the tenth. Lowman, one of our top clutch hitters, was at the plate. Victory seemed imminent. I told Jason that the first pitch would be a fastball down the middle, and that was what he got. He hit the ball to centerfield, looking like it would be deep enough for a sacrifice fly to score the winning run. Grove City's centerfielder made a great throw to cut down Brent Baker at the plate. We still had runners on second and third but our next hitter popped up. We went to the eleventh inning.

Again, we had to check our guts. The momentum had definitely shifted to Grove City's side. It seemed that they just kept doing whatever it took to keep us from winning. Ron Jones, their pitcher, had pitched the whole game for them, and he was still going strong after the eleventh. I kept telling our kids to keep fighting. Cannon kept their hitters off base, and we finally had another good chance to score in the twelfth inning.

Jones was still pitching well, but we managed to get something started. We had runners on first and third with one out with Baker at the plate. He entered the game as a defensive replacement, but it was his turn to come through offensively. Baker hit a ground ball to their first baseman, but it was too tough of a play to make. Brian Cutlip beat the throw to home plate, and we had broken the punch bowl. The 1998 championship was finally ours.

Our bench erupted out on to the field. I told Rob and R.J. that I really respected them and their kids and that what we took part in that day is the way baseball and competitive athletics are meant to be. There was a decent-sized crowd on hand that day that probably would agree.

I was tremendously happy for our kids. They worked hard and deserved it. They overcame adversity and never quit. It was a great comeback story not unlike my own. I felt a special bond with the kids on the team and we were really building something to be proud of. I believed that the championship season of 1998 would be followed by many more at Waynesburg.

We lost six of our last eight games and missed out the ECAC tournament, which is that level of baseball's equivalent to the NCAA basketball NIT. We established our first goal and the foundation was in place. I really thought that next year would be our year. We were losing only one senior, and although Adam Jack was a very important part of our team, every single player on the team would be better, and we would have new recruits that would make the team stronger.

The conference post-season awards were all ours. We had four first-team all-conference performers and two second-teamers. Adam was named player of the year, and I was the conference coach of the year. All the pain, suffering, depression, and despair I had gone through were worth it. Sleeping in three sweatshirts with no heat and washing my clothes in the shower didn't matter. All that mattered was how happy our players were after we won.

The kids bought a punch bowl and broke it at their post-game celebration. We all kept pieces of it. We had created many special memories in the short time that we were together. I told them that the next year we were going to take it one step farther and get to the NCAA tournament.

During the summer, I went about my business recruiting. We had commitments from a few great kids, and we were in the ballpark with a few others. I thought that with a couple more pieces, the puzzle would be complete.

The demands of the SID job were becoming difficult to me. I had little experience doing the layouts for the media guides although I easily handled the writing. Some of the students knew more about the layout aspect that we would need to use for the football team's media guide, which was an extensive project. One of the students, Jessica Hajek, was doing a great job and I relied on her heavily. I wanted to hire her to be my assistant for part-time wages and possibly even take over as SID herself. I couldn't do a good job anymore. I was too obsessed with baseball.

Out on the recruiting trail, I talked to other coaches about the situation I was in at the college. Most people agreed that it was hard to devote time to being a good college coach and fulfill the other requirements of the position. Many advised me to start looking around for another job. I thought about it, but what the kids were accomplishing at Waynesburg and the special relationship we had made me want to stay.

In July of 1998, I heard news that Dan Kubacki, a fine young coach in his own right, was leaving his position as head baseball coach at Youngstown State University. There were many people encouraging me to apply for the job, but I couldn't think about leaving the kids at Waynesburg or jeopardizing the great relationships I had with the people I worked for, especially Rudy and Richard. Those people meant a lot to me. I was looking forward to building a program at Waynesburg.

About that time, my desire was really dwindling as far as my SID duties. I was essentially working two full-time jobs and teaching two college level courses. We were also having trouble getting a commitment to have repairs and improvements made to the baseball field. I was having trouble looking at my living conditions every day, knowing that I deserved a better quality of life for doing a good job professionally.

People kept mentioning the opening at Youngstown State when I was scouting games. By the time August rolled around, I was mentioning the job to myself. I wondered if I could realize many coaches' dream of being a Division I college head coach. When I drove to Athens to recruit at the Ohio State American Legion Tournament, I made up my mind that I would apply for the job.

After the first night of tournament games, I had dinner with some other coaches and some scouts at Coach Carbone's house. When Coach Carbone asked me how everything was going at Waynesburg, I shared my concerns and recent discouragement with him. Before I could mention it, Coach Carbone read my mind.

"Hey, the job at Youngstown State is open," Coach Carbone said. "I'll call Jim Tressel."

Jim Tressel was the legendary football coach at Youngstown State and was also the school's executive director of athletics before he became the head football coach at Ohio State. He had been an assistant football coach at Ohio State for several years while Coach Carbone was an assistant baseball coach there.

"Do you know Jim Tressel?" I asked, wondering if God was now steering me in Youngstown State's direction.

"I know him well," Coach Carbone said. "Our offices were next to each other at Ohio State. I called him to recommend Kubacki."

I began to think I had a chance for the job. When I returned to Waynesburg, I talked to my father about the situation. He said he had done some work with Dr. Les Cochran, who was then Youngstown State's president. There was another strong connection.

Some of my friends in coaching helped me. Mark Stacy offered to call a former Youngstown State football coach, Jon Heacock, and asked him to put in a good word for me. Four or five other friends in coaching called the athletic administration at Youngstown.

One day in mid-August, I ran into Eric Meek at the mall in Steubenville. He was the head football coach at Wellsville High School, located just north of Steubenville. I knew him through Matt Morrison when they coached together at Toronto High School. Eric had spent a few years as an assistant football coach working for Coach Tressel at Youngstown State. He volunteered to make a call for me. A chance meeting turned into another good connection.

The Walkoskys were also helping me again. Dave had a friend on the Youngstown State football staff at the time who was able to relay information to me about the pace of the hiring process. Dave's older brother, Mike, had just taken a job in Youngstown with a company that was well-connected with the people in the athletic department at Youngstown State. Mike sent my resume to Coach Tressel through the people he worked for.

There were no guarantees that I would get the job, so I went back to business as usual at Waynesburg. There were a few recruits that I was trying to get to come to Waynesburg who were outstanding players. They had not made decisions as of early August, but I backed off, knowing in the back of my mind that I might leave for Youngstown State. Those kids chose other schools but I knew I did the right thing. I couldn't recruit them under the false pretense that I would stay.

The hiring process at Youngstown State was taking a long time. As we continued fall baseball at Waynesburg things started to become overwhelming with baseball, teaching, and my situation in the sports information department. I started to realize that I would likely leave for Youngstown State if the opportunity came.

Finally, the administrators from Youngstown State called me for an interview. They first asked Rudy if they could talk to me. Thanks to the great relationship Rudy and I had and his confidence in me, he gave me a great recommendation. The interview went as well as I thought it possibly could have. I was totally confident that if I was meant to be at Youngstown State I would be offered the job.

There were several other candidates who had to be interviewed. It would take a few more days, and a weekend was coming up before a decision would be made. I had to tell my players at Waynesburg because the rumors were starting to surface about my interest in Youngstown State. That was as hard as anything I ever had to do.

For almost a week, my professional career was in limbo. I wasn't sure if I had a job at either place. Rudy and I had a meeting to see what we could do about making the SID job more productive because I simply could not do it anymore. It was not technically under his supervision, but he wanted to help. He was curious as to what I had in mind to try to promote my assistant into the position.

"Mike, this is something that could greatly effect your status at the college," Rudy said.

"I am aware of that," I said. "I have every confidence that everything will work out for the better."

"Have you heard anything from Youngstown State?" Rudy asked.

"Not yet," I replied.

"I can't believe you're being so calm about this," Rudy said. "There is a lot at stake here for you. You're acting like James Bond."

We laughed, but I was fearful that I would never work for anyone again whom I respected as much and was as helpful to me as Rudy. He always took time to give me advice when I had problems, and I appreciated that. One of the things he helped me with was how strongly I believed in myself. Overcoming all that I had gone through was good for my peace of mind. I wasn't trying to act like James Bond but my faith, confidence, and prayers let me know everything would be all right.

After a few more long days, Coach Tressel called to offer me the job at Youngstown State. I accepted but I was dragging my feet. The contract would not be ready to sign for two weeks. I told Richard and our vice president who supervised athletics, Jerry Wood, two weeks before that I had a chance for another job but I would consider staying if the conditions of my job and contract would improve. After I talked with one of our vice presidents, it was clear to me that Waynesburg could not afford to keep me. I knew in my heart that I had to leave anyway. I never wanted to look back at a missed opportunity to be one of only 280-some Division I head baseball coaches in the country. I signed with Youngstown State to become one of the country's youngest Division I head baseball coaches at age 31.

# Chapter Nineteen

# All the Way on My Second Chance

# CHAPTER NINETEEN — ALL THE WAY ON MY SECOND CHANCE

I knew we would be in for a tough year in my first season at Youngstown State. Fortunately, I hired two great friends as assistant coaches to support me. George Powell came from Otterbein College, and Dennis Vince, a good friend of the family, were a big help in that tough first year. If we had played the Waynesburg team we expected to field for the 1999 season, Waynesburg would have beaten Youngstown State. The team at Waynesburg would change face immediately after my departure though. Some wanted to come with me to Youngstown State, others were disappointed that I left so they didn't return, and others who didn't like me came back to the team.

Several team members quit after I left. I didn't want them to quit but they were upset that I left. Several players I dismissed came back. I also wanted some of Waynesburg's players to come with me.

Bill Parcells, the great NFL coach, always made a priority to have "his" kind of guys on the teams he coached, no matter where he went. This is evidenced in the fact that players like Keith Byers, Jumbo Elliot, Curtis Martin, Dave Megget, and Pepper Johnson all played for at least two different organizations that were coached by Parcells at different times. If we were to get things going in the right direction at Youngstown State, I would have to do the same thing.

After all was said and done, only Jason Lowman and Brian McFarland would transfer to Youngstown State with me. There were at least seven players from Waynesburg that I wanted to come with me. There were a couple we didn't have room for at their positions on the roster, a couple who would be academically ineligible, and a couple who didn't want to come, but that is the way it was meant to be.

As I asserted my style and discipline, almost half of the kids would end up transferring out or just quitting the team at Youngstown State. Dan Kubacki was a great coach and a tough act to follow. Some of the players were intensely loyal to him and were not receptive to me. I was still convinced I was doing the right thing. To come to a team that had a 2.2 team grade point average and a 17-31 record and not try to change things would have been a terrible mistake. It is the hardest thing about coaching

194

but it has to be done. The resistance has ceased and our program continued to move forward.

I was fighting more than opposition from team members at first. In November of 1998, it was announced that Central Blood Bank in Pittsburgh was being investigated for faulty testing practices. I learned that some of the labs to which they sent their blood did not use proper testing techniques. There was a chance that anyone who had received blood from Central Blood Bank at different hospitals in the Pittsburgh area in the last several years could have received blood contaminated with AIDS, hepatitis, or any other disease that is transmissible through a blood transfusion. Included in this time frame was the blood I received the last time I was hospitalized in Presbyterian University Hospital right before my final surgery in October of 1996.

I was angry at first. "Why would you tease me with some promise in my life and pull the rug out from under me?" I asked God. For three days, I could barely concentrate on work or anything else. I thought about a possible lawsuit.

After a few days my anger subsided. I began to pray to God that the tests would be negative. Then I just put the situation in God's hands. I came to a great sense of calm, knowing that no matter what the test results were, everything would work out for the better. I had the test done the day after Thanksgiving and had three weeks to wait for the results.

Before the ostomy surgery, I would have gone crazy waiting for the results. The experiences I had been blessed with since then gave me a greater perspective on how little control I had over the events in my life. I could control only my reactions to those events. I thought about Brett Butler, the former major league outfielder, who was diagnosed with throat cancer several years before the end of his career. I remember seeing an interview once about the diagnosis, and he said he was angry at first. Then he simply prayed and said, "Show me the plan, Lord, show me the plan." He overcame cancer to return to the major leagues.

After Thanksgiving, I went back to work, knowing that no matter what the results, everything would somehow be fine. God's plan cannot be fought. Three weeks later the test results came back negative. It was a relief to get good news from a hospital for a change.

I had matured enough to put the situation in God's hands. From my experiences, I had found that there is no other way to get through such difficult times. I am fortunate because of my suffering to understand many things that I otherwise would not have known until I had left this earth. I know my mission is to teach baseball and pass along my experiences so others can learn and gain hope.

Everyone on earth has a mission. We are all blessed with special gifts and talents. If we discover these talents, cultivate them, and pursue our dreams of using those gifts with passion and integrity, we will make a successful contribution toward making the world a better place. Obstacles will always be a part of the equation, but if they are viewed as opportunities they can be overcome. I have an opportunity to be an example to people, demonstrating that many problems can be defeated no matter how severe they are or how long they last.

Another opportunity to overcome obstacles presented itself as my career continued at Youngstown State. We had done some good things in my first five seasons. Five players were drafted or signed by Major League Baseball teams, and we had several freshman All-American selections. We finished in the top half of our conference standings and made a name for ourselves in the Horizon League after we began playing in that league in 2002. Our team grade point average climbed to over 3.0. We successfully fundraised between $25,000 and $30,000 just to make ends meet for the program. Those achievements were not up to my standards though.

I began to feel really burned out by the time fall practice had begun in 2003. I thought we had assembled quite a team, but the support for the program had not grown enough. We had only 8.8 scholarships to divide among the whole team (most of our competitors had 11.7, the maxium for Division I baseball). Our budget was so small that our competitiveness was compromised because of our lack of resources. I had only part-time assistant coaches (all of the D-I schools we compete against had at least one full-time assistant and some of them had two). I was trying to just keep things together and keep us from embarrassing ourselves. I was doing much of the work with very little help and I was becoming frustrated because we had not won a championship. I seriously questioned whether we ever would with only about 60 percent of the resources we needed to survive. Sometimes that is the nature of being involved in a non revenue generating sport.

Many of my friends in coaching suggested that I look for another job. I felt like I was spending most of my time in what appeared to be a no-win situation. I was tired all of the time and the days were running into one another. I started to explore occupations outside coaching, and I was questioning the reason that God wanted me in this position. How was I ever going to be an example to people about overcoming adversity if I was not happy in my current situation?

By the time the 2004 spring season came around, I was physically, emotionally, and psychologically at the end of my rope. I could not think of a more trying way to open the season than the way we did, losing 13 of our first 15 games, all on the road. We lost many close games to several teams who had reached the NCAA tournament in 2003 or would do so in 2004. Some of our key pitchers suffered injuries early in the season and we couldn't hold leads.

The weather was also nasty. We would finish the year with 20 games either cancelled or rescheduled. Rain and snow seemed to follow us everywhere we went; from Chattanooga to Cincinnati to Milwaukee to Youngstown, we just couldn't seem to escape Mother Nature's wrath. More than one-fourth of our league games were cancelled due to weather, and we would finish the year with only 11 practices on a baseball field of some kind. But our guys hung tough and continued to compete, and their attitude and prayers were the only thing that sustained me.

Every night before I went to sleep, I took a knee and I thanked God for all the things that I had in my life: a healthy, happy family; the opportunity to be involved in baseball; to use that position to have a platform publicly speak about my story; and to live out God's plan for my life. The Bible says, *"This is the confidence we must have when approaching God; that anything we ask will be done if it is according to his will."* All season, I also continued to thank God in advance for helping us win the 2004 Horizon League championship.

That was very bold of me, to thank God in advance for helping us win that championship. But that is the confidence that I have in God, even though I was wondering if I could go on. I had numerous conversations with my parents and Dianne about being in total occupational despair. They kept me sane. To make matters worse, we struggled in conference play and finished dead last in the standings. Yet I would not give up and continued to keep the faith, the size of a grain of a mustard seed, that we could somehow win the conference tournament at the end of the season.

We finally started showing signs of life in the last few weeks of the season. We won a hard-fought, 12-inning mid-week game at home against Ohio U. when our senior first baseman, Jim Lipinski, hustled his way into a double to lead off the bottom of the twelfth. He was eventually driven in by another senior, catcher Adam Cox, to win the game, 7-6. Senior Kendall Schlabach had tied the contest in by driving in two runs with a two-out single in the bottom of the ninth.

That weekend we played the league's first place team, the University of Illinois at Chicago in a four game series at home. We continued to play well, winning three out of four games. That gave us confidence going into the last weekend of the regular season against another one of the league's best teams, Wisconsin-Milwaukee. But that whole series was washed out when rain drenched most of the upper midwest for a four-day period. I was somewhat concerned that we wouldn't be in a rhythm, especially offensively, when the conference tournament began a few days later on May 26.

Although we had the advantage of playing the entire tournament at our home stadium, beautiful Eastwood Field in Niles, Ohio, since we finished last in the standings, we would not be the home team for a single game in the double-elimination tournament. We would also have to play a tough Butler team in the opening round of the tournament.

We did have our number one pitcher, sophomore Justin Thomas, on the mound for us. That made me feel very confident, because Justin was having a great season. But so was Butler's left-handed pitcher Craig Costello, and he shut us out for the first eight innings of the game. Butler was able to score three runs to give them a decent lead going into the last inning. Things did not look very good, but I held on to that mustard seed's size of faith as we began the ninth inning.

We managed to get a few runners on base and scored a run, but we were down to our last out with the bases loaded. With two strikes in the count, sophomore Brandon Caipen drove in the tying runs with a clutch single, and then sophomore Charles Schultz drove in Caipen to give us a 4-3 lead. Freshman Andy Svitak pitched out of a one-out bases-loaded jam in the bottom of the ninth, and we had a dramatic, opening-round comeback win to start the tournament.

We beat Cleveland State in the second game, 7-2, behind a great pitching performance by sophomore Eric Shaffer. The stage was set for the winner's bracket final game against UIC. I felt incredibily relaxed and I was not nervous at all. I simply placed everything in God's hands and watched our guys go to work on a sunny Saturday afternoon.

A great crowd showed up to watch junior Chris Dennis take the mound for us. Chris had pitched a brilliant three-hit shutout against UIC when they were at our staduim a few weeks earlier, and we felt UIC would have trouble hitting him. We jumped on UIC early, scoring three runs in the top of the first inning. But Chris had trouble finding the strike zone and would eventually walk 11 UIC hitters, and they would tie the game 4-4. UIC would strand 16 runnners in the contest, and we would strand 12, combining for a Horizon League tournament record. Both teams came close to scoring every inning when we didn't score. The game was back and forth the whole day.

UIC's shortstop, Jordan DeVoir, made several outstanding plays to take base hits away from our hitters. Lipinski made several strong defensive plays to do the same to their hitters, and senior Frank Santore pitched out of a bases-loaded jam in relief in the sixth to stop another scoring threat. We thought all was lost the next inning when UIC's top hitter, Mike Hughes, came to the plate with two runners on and two out and drilled a line drive into the left-center gap, but Schlabach came out of nowhere to make a spectacular diving catch to end that rally. We finally pushed across a run in the top of the ninth, and Svitak earned the win by pitching a scoreless bottom half of the ninth, to give us a 5-4 win. Some people in the crowd and involved with the teams called it the most intense baseball game they had ever seen. I couldn't say I disagree, but I was relaxed the whole time, just placing things in God's hands, and knowing that I had been through tougher things than winning an intense baseball game.

The stage was set for the championship game the next day, and May 30, 2004, is one day I will never forget. It was 70 degrees and there was not a cloud in the sky. A crowd of over 1,000 people, the most we ever had, were on hand to watch us play Cleveland State, who had beaten UIC immediately after we did to get to the championship game. We were relaxed because Cleveland State would have to beat us twice, and we would only have to win one game.

On the mound we had sophomore Kevin Libeg, a hometown standout from nearby Hubbard, Ohio, who took control of the game early. Our bats were alive, and we pounded out 14 hits and scored ten runs. Senior Clint Ford, who had struggled with injuries for the past two years, hit a big home run to get the offense going. Libeg pitched seven strong innings to get the win. Seniors Mike Hosterman and Paul Yates closed the story-book game out, and we had a 10-1 championship game victory.

The scene of the whole day was almost surreal. I had visualized exactly what happened when I had prayed each night for months preceding the event. As the trophies were passed out to our players on the field, I began to search for my parents in the stands. They were the ones who stood by me though thick and thin, and they were responsible for my still being alive, let alone being a Division I champion. I finally found my mom, and we shared a long embrace and she cried. I wanted to say thanks for so many things, but I was was so choked up I couldn't speak. I thought about Mario Lemieux and Michael Jordan breaking down and crying tears of relief after they had won their respective championships. Those tears were at the top of my throat, but I kept them on the inside. As I found my father and hugged him, I thought about all the hospitals, tests, surgeries, and the pain. I began to smile because I had been reminded again that suffering had allowed my faith to strengthen me, and that I could overcome any obstacles.

The NCAA selection committee paired us against the University of Texas, the top-ranked team in the tournament, for the regional. Texas was every bit as good as advertised and they beat us, 10-3. We were eliminated by TCU in the next game of the tournament, but I kept things in perspective. We had a monumental achievement we were bringing home, and we had evoked a great deal of pride for the school and the city. It was a strong reminder to me that the most important thing in life is to never give up. All the pain and suffering I went through with Crohn's and the surgeries will be far greater than most of the bad things that will come my way.

I don't want to scare anyone with Crohn's disease or ulcerative colitis. The chances are miniscule of having symptoms as severe as I had. I had asked Dr. Graham how severe she thought my case of Crohn's was. She rated it at least a nine on a scale of one to ten. I guess ten would be close to death. Dr. Thomas said that I had the worst case of

Crohn's disease he had seen in 30 years of treating patients with intestinal illnesses. His associates concurred.

For me to be able to overcome such a severe case of a devastating disease is a testament to all of the people who helped me, especially my family. It is also a testament to the strong will that God has blessed me with. I feel fortunate to have been blessed with the skills and the opportunity to be in such a select group of Division I coaches. I am happy to show people that we are all capable of overcoming tremendous odds if we try hard enough and have faith. Anything is possible with God.

If I can overcome the things I have experienced and consider myself a better person, maybe others who are suffering can experience the same miracle in their lives. I was not healed. I was not able to avoid the surgery that I so feared. My miracle was that I had a change of my perception of a situation that I feared more than death.

Barbara Walters asked Stevie Wonder about the chances of gaining his sight through a new surgical procedure. His hopes were very grounded, and his realistic answer was indicative of how strong his faith is.

*"If it is God's will, the miracle will happen and I will see,"* Wonder told Walters. *"If not, miracles are still happening in my life."*

I have learned to appreciate the miracles in my life much more. I thank God every day for choosing me to live out the plan of overcoming not only Crohn's disease but also overcoming my emptiness and misunderstanding of life before the illness and depression during the toughest times. I am lucky.

I tell anyone I talk to who is having a bout with depression to seek help right away. It happens to many people. According to the Harvard Medical School's *Family Health Guide*, one in five American adults will have been depressed at one time or another in his or her life. I believe it is normal to experience extended sentiments of sadness during life's trials. In retrospect, I should have had much better treatment for my depression, and it is only by the miracle of God's will that I am still on earth. I urge anyone who is depressed and thinking morbid thoughts not to let it go untreated. I believe that when people suffer through desperate times, it is common to feel like giving up, but only for a very short time. When those thoughts become repetitive, it is time to see a psychologist or psychiatrist. They help many people gain strength and perspective about coping with life's ups and downs. Prayers will help but God helps those who help themselves.

One of America's greatest leaders, Abraham Lincoln, battled many maladies including depression, throughout the course of his life. He overcame them to change history. He spoke about overcoming adversity:

*In this sad world of ours, sorrow comes to all and it often comes with bitter agony. Perfect relief is not possible, except with time. You cannot believe now that you will ever feel better, but this is not true. You are sure to be happy again. Knowing this, truly believing it, will make you less miserable now. I have had enough experience to make this statement.*

I couldn't agree with this statement more. Time heals wounds. I found out the hard way that if someone is sick or depressed, a doctor must be seen quickly to get help. Modern medicine doesn't have all the answers. It can be very frustrating to a patient. Medicine can help people get back on their feet, as do alternative health care practitioners. I believe they must be used in conjunction with one another to combat chronic conditions.

Friends and family are also necessary to fight disease and depression. Disease often leads to isolation and loneliness, and then depression has a chance to thrive. People who are sick can feel very alone and that no one understands what they are going through. Sometimes support groups are not attractive because each person had a different life before his or her illness. Each person also has a different set of expectations of what life will be like after being faced with a health crisis. Support groups can be hard to find relief in because each person is a complex being with many psychological, sociological, biological, and historical factors that make up its symptoms, and how to cope. They are most aware of the depth of the trauma that is suffered by one of their loved ones being diagnosed with a debilitating condition. Sometimes they are the best support groups. The sick person would surely help a loved one if the loved one is suffering. Sick people cannot be too proud to reach out and grab hold of the helping hands that are extended to them. I have had enough experience to make this statement.

Support groups, however, can be of great help. They can direct patients to the right doctors and hospitals that are more adept than others at treating certain conditions. They offer people a chance to relieve the pent-up anger and frustration that accompanies disease. People can see in support groups that they are not alone and often find that there are people who have suffered just as terribly but have risen above the odds to lead productive, happy lives. Sometimes witnessing that and knowing it is amongst the most important steps toward recovery.

As the book of Proverbs says, *"As a man thinketh in his heart, so is he."* If one witnesses the recovery of others, it is proven that it can be done, and a sick person will receive not only some hope but also some inspiration. I believed I would recover, so I did. I am not sure what would have happened to me were it not for Merril, Diane, Elaine, and others who helped me. I knew that if they had recovered, I could, too.

Sometimes I wonder if my newly determined inspiration is just a reflex action to reaching rock bottom. I do realize, though, that the only reason that I fought back from eight devastating flare-ups was that I had faith all along. Deep inside I knew God had a plan for me just as there is one for every person. I am here for a reason just as everyone else is.

I have summoned the courage to speak publicly and write about all of the bad things that have happened to me. I hope that others can benefit from my mistakes. My story is indicative of how much one's life can turn around as long as the smallest bit of faith is present.

It must be understood that my case of IBD was one of the worst imaginable. My hope is not that people with IBD will fear that they will experience the tremendous suffering that I did, rather, that those with IBD will see that someone has overcome such great odds and that they can, too. All people can also see from my story that alcohol and material achievements are no way to help self-esteem. There is greatness in each person that is created in God's likeness on this earth, no matter who they are or what they do. When at such low points, it is hard to have faith in this concept.

The Bible says all that is needed is a bit of faith the size of a grain of a mustard seed. Many times, my faith was this small. I often wondered why God would give me so much to overcome. I remember what Mother Teresa once said, *"God never gives us more than we can handle. Sometimes, I wish He wouldn't trust us so much."*

I wouldn't trade the experiences I have had for anything. I could choose to be bitter, but I would rather see the glass as half full rather than half empty. Lou Gerhrig, the great New York Yankee first baseman and one of my all-time heroes, called himself "the luckiest man on the face of the earth." He said these words as he stood in Yankee Stadium, dying from the disease that now bears his name, also known as amyotrophic lateral sclerosis.

I consider myself lucky, too. Like Lance Armstrong, I am going all the way on my second chance. When I think of all the great people who helped me, like my parents, Dr. Thomas, Dr. Graham, Coach Carbone, Elaine, Merril, Dianne, Richard, the Walkoskys, and so many others, I know that I received many more than two chances. God sent those people into my life at times when I needed them most. Those encounters and their timing were not coincidences. This disease was sent into my life when I needed it the most.

The whole ordeal has made me a stronger, better, more appreciative person. It has shown me what the love of God, family, and friends really means. We are inundated with negative acts that are sometimes glorified because of the publicity they receive. I know through all of the people who have reached out to me that acts of kindness still outnumber bad things that happen.

Bad things will happen to everyone. It is not necessarily the bad things that happen to someone but how we cope with them. Through adversity, we discover our true character. I am grateful for the bad things that happened to me. It is a matter of perspective. I have learned to take negative situations and make positives out of them. Had I never become ill, I would not be in a position to help people as I am now.

I am not normal. No one is. I had to sink to the lowest conceivable circumstances to realize that I have special gifts to give, as everyone does. I also have come to realize that I do not have to be perfect and that everything and everyone are filled with perfect imperfections, as Wayne Dyer says. I discuss high-school players almost every day with my assistant coaches. I catch myself talking about a potential recruit who may have many skills, but one area may be lacking. He can do this and that, but can he run? Or can he hit with power? Then I say to myself, I wouldn't ask whether or not Cindy Crawford could cook. No one is perfect, especially not me. It is better to stress the positive things.

There are so many positive things in my life now that I cannot count them. My relationships with God, my family, friends, and coworkers are much better than I ever could have hoped. I am extremely active. Being a Division I head coach requires an average of over 60 working hours per week. We travel all around the country, playing games and recruiting. I throw about 200 pitches of batting practice twice weekly to my team, and I hit them ground balls and fly balls until they are tired of chasing them. My golf game is okay, and I convince myself that it will be better if I ever find more time to play. I lift weights five to six times a week. I even studied martial arts with Merril for a short time. I do all these things with a passion I never thought I had until it was brought out by overcoming this disease.

I did not like the person I was at all before I was diagnosed with this horrible disease, and while I was so ill and in denial, I never really loved anyone or anything because I never loved myself. The path my life was on was one of physical, emotional, spiritual, and social destruction. I am a contributor now. I would rather be known for what I give than what I acquire. I am able to at least attempt to see the good things in every person and every situation I encounter and try to stay positive even during the toughest circumstances. I would never have done that before. This is why I believe that seeing the worst set of circumstances come to fruition in my life was actually the best thing that ever happened to me. **I am now healthier than normal.**

# Resources

**RESOURCES:  RELATED ASSOCIATIONS AND CONTACT INFORMATION**

**United Ostomy Association**
19772 McArthur Boulevard, Suite 200
Irvine, CA 92612
(800) 826-0826    www.uoa.org

**Coloplast Ostomy Supplies**
Coloplast Corp.
1955 West Oak Circle
Marietta, GA   30062-2249
(770) 281-8400

**Crohn's and Colitis Foundation of America**
386 Park Avenue South, 17th Floor
New York City, New York 10020
(212) 685-3440
(212) 779-4098
(800) 343-3637   www.ccfa.org

**National Digestive Diseases Information Clearinghouse**
2 Information Way
Bethseda, MD 20892-3570
Phone:  (800) 891-5389 or (301) 654-3810
Fax: (301) 907-8906
E-Mail: nddic@info.nddk.nih.gov

**National Center for Complementary and Alternative Medicine Clearinghouse**
P.O. Box 8218
Silver Spring, MD 20892
(888) 644-6226
www.nccam.nih.gov

**Digestive Health & Nutrition Magazine**
American Gastroenterological Association
7910 Woodmont Avenue, 7th Floor
Bethseda, MD 20814
(301) 654-2055  www.dhn-online.org

**International Association for Medical Assistance to Travelers**
417 Center Street
Lewiston, NY 14092
(716) 754-4883  www.sentex.net/~iamat

**Equal Opportunity Employment Commission**
1801 L. Street, NW
Washington, DC 20507
(800) 669-4000  www.eeoc.gov

**American Psychiatric Association**
100 Wilson Boulevard Suite 1825
Arlington, Va. 22209-3901
(703) 907-7300
toll-free: (888) 35-psych (357-7924)  www.pysch.org

**American Pyschological Association**
750 First Street NE
Washington, DC 2002-4242
(202) 336-5500
toll free: (800) 374-2721  www.apa.org

**National Mental Health Association**
2001 North Beauregard Street 12th Floor
Alexandria, Va. 22311
toll free: (800) 969-NMHA  (969-6642)
www.nmha.org

**For further information on depression see:**
www.depression.com

# Special Thanks

Special thanks to Mel Helitzer of the Ohio University journalism department, Richard Krause of the Waynesburg College department of communication, and my editor, Diane Wilding, for their guidance and encouragement.

To my technical advisors: Mark Bercik of America Sports Publishing, Mario Saggio, Brian Blasko, and Thom Foley. Your advice and expertise have amazed me and kept this book moving in the right direction: Tracey Bodnar of Wild Ink Mouse Productions, John Moliterno of Allegra Printing, Bob Yosay of the *Youngstown Vindicator*, and Carl Leet for their great artwork and design.

To my good friends who stayed in my corner and pulled me back into coaching: Gregg Bahen, Mark Stacy, Matt Morrison, Joe Carbone and Dave Walkosky. You are all tremendous coaches but even better people.

To the great doctors who helped put me back together again: Dr. Fred Thomas, Dr. Toby Graham, and Dr. Ken Lee. All the time, blood, sweat, and tears you have put into your craft is matched only by your compassion and competence. I was fortunate to have you improve my life just as you have for countless others.

To my guardians who became shining beacons of light: Dianne Burkhart, Merril Hudson, and especially Elaine Hagerty. I fear to think where I would be without you. Anyone who has had the pleasure of knowing you fully realizes the presence of God here on earth.

Most important: to God and to my parents, Barb and Ed Florak. How can I quantify in words the gratitude for not only creating my life but also later saving it?

# How to Contact the Author

*Healthier than Normal*

---

To order more copies of *Healthier than Normal*, contact

Mike Florak

At

www.MikeFlorak.com

1-888-4 FLORAK

1-888-435-6125

or write to

## Mike Florak

P.O. Box 2547

Wintersville, OH 43953